hey hey
EVERYDAY

ELIZABETH MAE, FNTP

Photos by Michelle Sharkey
Special Photos by Becky Jones
Illustrations by Brad Golliher
Design by Oliver Creative

For Truman and Calvin.

You're the best motivation for healing myself, this home, our neighbors and the world. Grateful to be called "Momma". Endlessly thankful to be grown and shaped by your love and friendship. You are the best guys I know.

Bojangles, Momma

ACKNOWLEDGEMENTS

To my health that fell apart and the stress and destruction that made it all possible - I thank you - a hopeless thing has become a proliferative agent for health. What a gift.

This book has come together, in part, thanks to my many clients who have trusted me with their health and their children's health. I learn something new in every client's care and am compelled to make these recipes so we can all serve up something healing and sustainable. Thank you for trusting me.

Abby O' Leary should get a high five from us all for heading the project, sourcing all the needs, keeping me going and communicating among all the parties. And being extremely patient. You. Are. The. Best.

Michelle Sharkey knocked these photos out of the ballpark, was a saint about my country music choices on shoot days and sourced so many awesome dishes and materials. You're better than you know and I'll tell everyone, forever!

Scott and Hope Newell, thank you for opening your home to my wild idea - appreciate it so much! Sorry about the spoons.

B-rad (Bradley Golliher) thanks for being rad and designing so many fun, encouraging graphics that my clients enjoy each day they're in care. Big hugs for letting us use them in and through this book.

So grateful for talented photo-day kitchen prep support. Winona Eargle is responsible for any pretty picture in the green kitchen and for my clothes being styled properly. Karol Langley brought the cheer, the beautiful cauliflower pan and all the chill to shoot day 2. Abby Siever came in hot with groceries, encouragement, pep and all the laughs for shoot day 3. On shoot day 4, Sophia Brown learned to love beets, supported me constantly, made recipe edits and was so fun to be with. Brie Golliher, who's long been the most supportive bestie, came to cheer on shoot day 4, make pictures, prep food for giving and spent the night loving on my boys because of a snow storm. Bless each of you for supporting my marathon days of cooking. Thank you!!

Big thanks to my parents. My Momma, Penny, crafted several of these recipes or experimented with me as we recreated family favorites for my body's new way of life. Bigger thanks for cooking with "little me" and instilling a love and knowledge of food in me early. Thanks to my Dad, for teaching me the difference between Black Seeded Simpson lettuce and Bibb lettuce and the value of Vidalia onions - my love of gardening and salads came from all the hours we spent planting and I spent weeding - ha!

Jenn and English - you're the best practitioner, daily cheer squad a girl could ask for. Wouldn't wanna Hey Hey without y'all. To the vast Tampa FNTP class of 2019 - I love you all. Girls trip, for real.

Bestie Becky - you're the real MVP - thanks for having my back and offering your life and home to my boys and my healing season. For cheering loudest, making reels and shooting so many pictures that helped me launch Hey Hey Mae: you're the bestest. You helped put me back together." to the end.

Rye, thanks for having my back, prepping my chicken salad, making my tea and reminding me you're proud and I can do it all if I wanna. Grateful's just a start.

Tru and Cal - you've been the best taste testers, dishwasher unloaders and honest feedback givers. Thanks for encouraging me, calling me to more and reminding me that Hey Hey Holiday needs to get underway.

I can't believe I got to make this tool I've been dreaming of. Thank you for reading.

TABLE OF CONTENTS

DISCLAIMER

Hey Hey Mae LLC and Elizabeth Mae Sharrett have designed this book to provide information and recipes in regard to the subject matter covered. This book is sold with the understanding that the author is not liable for the misconception or misuse of the information provided. The purpose of this book is to educate, and in no way to treat, diagnose or prevent disease. The information presented herein is in no way intended as a substitute for medical or nutrition counseling. The author does not assume medical or legal liability for the use or misuse of the information contained in this book.

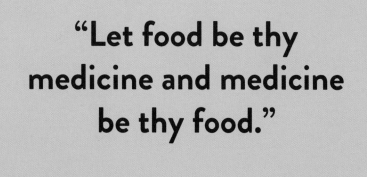

"Let food be thy
medicine and medicine
be thy food."

"Health is the greatest
of human blessings."

All attributed to the "Father of Medicine,"
the originator of "either help or do no harm", Hippocrates.
May we, in large part, return to this simplicity.

PART 1

heyhey

HOW TO CHANGE YOUR LIFE WITH FOOD: SIMPLY

INTRODUCTION

hey hey, I'm so glad you're here. Whether you're just dipping your toes into food as medicine or you're pulling your hair out trying to feed five different special diets under one roof — you're in the right place. This book is an overflow of my day-to-day transition into eating to build health. My health crashed after my second son was born, as my family's life was rapidly changing.

Within a matter of months, I'd lost 80 pounds, struggled to get around and care for my boys and was neck deep in implementing change as a solo mom. Solo momming is not a focus of mine — but in the words of a favorite client *"when following protocols are hard or cooking dinner in this better way feels like a lot, I remind myself 'Elizabeth does this by herself — I've got this!'"* And you absolutely do! Whether you're a solo parent recovering health after a destructive marriage ended, a special needs caregiver or a person who simply considers their relationship with food their biggest hurdle: you've got this.

You **can** take back control of your health. One day at a time, your household can promote curiosity and power around health, replacing fear and struggle. Our bodies were designed to heal! You have been gifted the ritual of food — three times a day, even — and food's communal power for healing is there anytime you want to employ it for the food of building health. The biggest lesson I've learned through my health crisis, parenthood and the everyday ebb and flow of life is: your life is as good as the story you tell yourself. The way we think about food, matters.

Food can easily be a miserable thing you have to do over and over again. *"These kids have to eat THREE times a day AND 235 snacks?"* Or, meal preparation can be the shoulder-to-shoulder time you get to hear from your teen. Dinners at home can yield that quiet Mom and Dad time at the sink, while you catch up - washing and drying, device-free. Weekday meals can be a nourishing practice that makes space and leaves energy for hosting a restful Sunday backyard dinner with friends and family.

Know what all three of these meal preparation stories have in common? The healing power of community and relationship. The trump card for all human restoration is relationship. More than food, you may ask? I've watched client after client make amazing headway when food is changed, then it is relationship and relational health that makes it all stick. I've come to see, that while food sustained me and gave me a life back, the relationships I was steeped in and loved by, put me back together and made the work stick. The community phase of healing is where my autoimmune diseases found remission.

How will you push back the nutrition information overwelm and know which nutrition info to keep and which to toss? We'll work together to establish simple food guides that are easy enough for your preschooler to remember. You'll learn the shorthand of how your body works and how best to nourish it. Easily. Daily. Together, we'll build a simple kitchen you can enjoy cooking in. I want to encourage you to usher joy into your kitchen as you provide nourishment to your body and your family's bodies. We're simplifying each "learning" foundation of cooking for health to make them memorable, eventually making meal planning and cooking, possible from memory. Remember the stories that you create around your kitchen time can grow your affections for the time you spend there. What a privilege to nourish people so they can go forth to do what they were made for! One skill and recipe at a time. One meal at a time.

My sweetest memories with my grandmothers were around food: fetching sauerkraut from the basement or being greeted with a pan of brownies. Holidays were day after day in the kitchen with my Mom and sisters, making hundreds of cookies for giving. Each day, we build these relational ties to food with our families. This cookbook is also the culmination of my struggle against the emotional work of swapping rich family recipes for ones that fit my healing diet. When I made changes, I knew I couldn't let food sensitivities dictate the way I'd learned to feed my family. I didn't want to give up Saturday waffles or snow day chicken soups. So we won't.

I come from a long line of women without recipes and a longer line of kitchen busybodies. In this book, I'll share some of my tried and true favorites that I find myself making again and again. I want to encourage you to play around with the recipes. Modify in ways that work for your family, and get creative — most recipes have flexible tips and tricks to change them for various diets or bulk them up for hungrier eaters. I've added in some alternatives and tips for various food sensitivities or modifications, but if your family has a unique flavor tradition for a dish - try that and be sure to share with me — I love seeing you get creative in the kitchen!

Finally, get your kids involved and teach them how to nourish their body too — you might even find they are more excited to eat when they've helped you cook. The simple food rules laced throughout are health building tools for both their relationship with

their bodies and their plates.

Trick one: get a really good knife for chopping veggies and have some fun!

"YOU CAN TAKE BACK CONTROL OF YOUR HEALTH. ONE DAY AT A TIME. OUR BODIES WERE DESIGNED TO HEAL!"

WHO IS HEY HEY AND
WHAT I BELIEVE

Hey, hey, I'm Mae...but you'll be calling me Elizabeth. Mae is my middle name, a tribute to my grandmother, Gladys, who taught me how to care for my people through food. After a few years of health decline and health building through food, I went to school to learn the science behind what made my healing possible.

I am a Functional Nutritional Therapy Practitioner (FNTP) with further training in labwork, GI healing, the art of hormone balance, functional blood chemistry, bioindividual nutrition and pediatric nutritional therapy. I rely on foods and nutraceuticals to bring healing....but for them to work: **WE MUST HAVE A FUNCTIONAL PERSPECTIVE.**

I start every care process with these questions:
1. How does the body **function**?
2. What is the root of the **dysfunction**?
3. How do we give the body what it needs to restore that **function**?

I've been through my own share of care, I've been in your shoes, and I wrote this book because I wish I had a simple, everyday guide when I started on my nourishing journey.

If you're holding this book, I anticipate you may be beginning care, too, with a trusted practitioner. Or you may just be beginning to take back control of your health. **I'm here, celebrating you for investing in your own tomorrow!**

I am truly so excited for this season of your life. This work changed my life. It wiped my sick body off the floor and allowed me to not only care for my children, but have a clear mind to learn the scientific magic behind what happened in my healing.

I want freedom and life for you. And I know every dollar and every minute spent chopping veggies is worth it.

I hope you find this to be the ultimate guide to setting yourself up for nutrient dense meals, nourishing your body to balanced blood sugar, while keeping everyday really simple and enjoyable.

This is gonna be the best! Let's think about where we're going. Where do you want to be in 3 months? 6 months? You are doing exactly what you need to be to see big, big changes in your health, disposition, energy and joy! I promise — I've lived it!!

I hope this book becomes so basic to you that over time, you feel so comfortable in the kitchen you rarely need to pick it up, except to remember a measurement or recall a few favorite meals.

I want to teach you how to cook in a formula-type way — where you can select a protein, a couple veggies, and a sauce to bring together a few meals from one batch of cooking. My hope is that as you learn the foundations of nourishing eating that you are even inspired to create a few of your own creations and combinations (if you do, share with me — I want to see!)

For those with food fears or anxieties and problematic health that effects your daily life. For starters: if you aren't certain your digestive tract is functioning in top condition, I hope you reach out to a reputable practitioner who can create a bio-individual plan for you.

We need your digestive tract functioning if we want to heal through nutrition. You can only absorb and use the nutrients you digest!

How do we heal digestion?
We heal the symptom load. All of those pesky symptoms need to reduce over time to create healing that sticks. They also each teach us something, or are a specific sign from a particular system in your body.

How does this happen with food? A couple things...

1. **Ancestral principals:** Remove processed foods and focus on nutrient-dense foods, eating healthy animal meats nose-to-tail, lessen toxin load, repair nutrient deficiencies, practice healthy eating habits, incorporate fermented foods and more.
2. **Remove nutrient depleting foods**: Rancid oils, trans-fats, synthetic foods, processed sugars and foods containing them, toxins like the synthetic vitamins in fortified foods etc.

What if food isn't or hasn't been enough yet?
That's ok — it isn't for many who have received diagnoses like IBS, IBD, diverticulitis or autoimmune diseases. Or for those who have experienced health challenges for many years.

This is where functional nutrition really shines: work with a practitioner, when you can, to improve your digestion if you need more of a boost than a special diet has to offer: bio-individual care is imperative!

We have stronger tools, like labs, which view your results through tighter, functional ranges to indicate early dysfunction. Technology allows us to view good and bad gut bacteria through stool testing. Many folks simply need a "food supercharging" through nutraceutical supplementation therapy, for a season, to strategically launch the body into its next level of healing.

After all, I've yet to be able to eat a pound of beets in a day, but sometimes those beet-based, gallbladder supports are all you need to end gallbladder symptoms.

BASIC KITCHEN SUPPLIES

My top favorites that make prepping a breeze:

A really sharp knife — Use for chopping all veggies. A sharp knife will change your meal prep life.

Serrated knife — Use this for cutting tomatoes, bread, butternut squash, etc.

A paring knife — Use for cutting up fruits.

A nylon serrated knife — Great to hand off to kids and get them involved in food prep, having a knife that can't cut them will give you peace of mind. Getting kids involved gives them a sense of ownership that they've contributed to the meal and are more excited to try new foods. The more we make food into play: the happier their story around food and eating will be.

Kitchen shears – Hella sharp, I use them to cut apart chicken and herbs. For safety, I prefer the ones that store in 2 pieces: usually hard enough for little hands to get together quick enough to cause any trouble before I can step in. That's a pro tip, for sure.

A colander — Love one with smaller holes and love a very large one for holding big greens like collards and kale.

A few cutting boards — I prefer a mix of sizes and materials and always a sanitizable option for raw meats. We keep some small boards in fun, colorful shapes that excite the boys for chopping fruits and veggies on their own for snacks.

Large & small mixing bowl — We use them a ton for prepping and mixing, toss all the chopped veggies in one. Some prefer to buy these with coordinating lids, so they'll double as storage.

Trash bowl — Use this to throw scraps you can use for making stock later, or compost / feed for chickens.

Mason jars — Really easy food storage, great for mixing up dressings, immersion blending mayo and sauces, storing clean veggies, storing leftovers, etc.

Plastic mason jar lids — I pop these on sauces, cut veggies and prepared fruits. The lids and bands drive me a little nuts, though they're great, too!

Lemon juicer and canning funnel — I make use of mason jars for storage, prepping, using the immersion blender in and drinking from. They're affordable, plentiful and

strong. This lemon juicer and canning funnel fit on top of the mason jars, are really handy and dishwasher safe.

Stackable Pyrex — Great for larger food storage. Stackable and rectangular keeps your fridge feeling organized and spacious. Glass storage greatly reduces toxin exposure.

Parchment paper on cookie sheet — Easy clean up for those sheet pan dinner nights or when roasting veggies. A must for any aluminum sheet pans, ok to pass on if you've invested in stainless steel pans.

12" and 8" cast iron pans — Cast iron's the MVP - on my stove all day, easy to re-heat dinner for lunch, can go from stove to oven. I also keep a few 8" cast iron pans for making Dutch babies, cornbread and quick flatbreads.

I won't tell anyone if you press the oatmeal after school cookie dough in the bottom of an 8" to whip up a skillet cookie. Just be sure you top it with my simple ice cream — in fact, I implore this as a **MUST** on your first weekend night of cleaner eating.

Prep and chop —Everything being clean and ready to pull from the fridge is key, so any other helps that make prepping a breeze for you are a must. Some friends love a simple, manual food chopper.

Dish towels —I prefer to use dish towels instead of paper towels for most kitchen jobs because they're reusable, can easily mop up excess water from produce washing and can be tossed under a cutting board for traction and stability when cutting tricky foods like a large watermelon or hard squash.

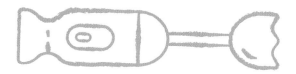

GADGETS WORTH HAVING:

Silicone basting brush — A must for greasing the waffle iron between waffles and a great help for getting all of the roasted veggies or BBQ covered in their respective sauces and seasonings.

Turkey baster — For dousing your roast chicken in its own nutritious juices.

Ice cream scoop — Easy to scoop meatballs or melons, I keep a variety of sizes to portion out smaller after school cookies or serve up a generous celebratory ice cream scoop.

Digital instant read meat thermometer — For years I didn't feel comfy cooking meat due to food safety fears — this removes the guesswork and makes meat-anything, a breeze.

Food processor — For making pesto, pie crusts and mixing. I also **LOVE** to use this when shredding the week's slaws and salads. So quick and a great "powertool" my boys enjoy using in the kitchen.

Immersion blender — This hand blender really easily makes sauces, soups & mayonnaise. Be sure to grab one with a detachable lower half to make cleanup fast.

Spiralizer — I love to bulk spiralize zucchini, carrots, potato and more. Varied shapes and textures make vegetables more appealing to the palate, I like a spiralizer with 3 blade options.

Vitamix — Super high powered blender, for sauces, soups, marinades. You can even use it to blend up muffins/pancakes and then just pour into muffin tins, etc.

Smooth edge can opener — Another place for kids to help! Any task that kids can complete entirely alone, is one that builds fun and confidence - we people love those feel-good tasks!

You can see a current, updated page of my favorite buys at www.heyheymae.com/kitchenfaves.

FOOD BUZZWORD
BREAKDOWN

The next big food trend is hitting the grocery shelf and you haven't even wrapped your head around the last set of food abbreviations or taglines? I know that food buying and terms can all get a little confusing... GMO, Organic, Grass-fed, pasteurized, plant based, Ketogenic, etc. There are loads of terms — some regulated, many not — and I want to clear it all up. Familiarized yourself with these, so that buzzwords become so familiar to you, you don't need this guide and can buy from any store or market with confidence. Walk with me as we work toward reading our packages for a more clear understanding!

FOOD TERMS

GMO
Genetically Modified Organism (GMO). GMO's are foods that have been altered in some way that does not occur naturally, by way of biotechnology. In order to produce something that is genetically modified, one organism gets spliced with another and some genes are altered or removed so the plant has the desired outcome.

For example, you could create herbicide resistance, resistance to frost and even lengthen the shelf life of foods. Common GMO crops include corn, soybeans, canola, squash, papaya, and salmon.

ORGANIC
Organic describes foods that are certified to the standards of the National Organic Program. This is a legally regulated program with a series of laws dictating plant and animal practices and production.

Organic foods are required to be grown without synthetic fertilizers, pesticides, fungicides, or any food additives. Organic agriculture focuses on the health of the soil as well as the health of the animal or the plant. All organic foods can also be traced back from a finished product to the seed or the animal.

GRASS-FED
Grass-fed indicates animals that have a natural diet consisting of grass and mainly grass — cattle, bison, lamb or goats can naturally eat only grass. You can also ask your local farmer if this animal has been Grass-finished. Grass-finished means the animal ate grass for most, but not all of their life — there could have also been supplemental feed right before they head to the butcher. Supplemental feed is used to put weight on an animal, more quickly.

The "best" term to look for when buying the highest quality Grass-fed meat is 100% Grass-fed. This indicates an animal that has eaten only grass its whole life long. No grain used at any point. These animals are rotationally grazed, exposed to a large amount of soil and microbes, which then pass on this nutrient density to the consumer.

CAGE-FREE
Cage-free is another trendy term, unregulated, too. We're talking about poultry. In many cases, hens aren't housed in cages, they are housed in huge barns. This means these animals aren't seeing the light of day, have no access to sunshine, fresh bugs and the like. It's a small, humane improvement, but doesn't mean much. Cage free is the "good" when buying poultry.

FREE-RANGE
Free-range describes poultry that has had access to the outside but are not required to go outside. This could simply mean that the chicken barn has open doors on it but the chickens don't go outside or that they have a small porch to go onto. Free-Range is the "better" when buying poultry.

PASTURE-RAISED
Poultry and pigs aren't able to live on grass alone. Pasture-raised or pastured means animals get to navigate the fields and forage and feed off a variety of nutrients — bugs, grasses, etc. — throughout the pasture. They live in the sunshine, soaking up vitamin D into their fat and eggs, enjoying microbes from

rotational grazing. Pasture-raised or pastured is the "best" when buying poultry.

HUMANELY RAISED

These are animals who are raised with a certain standard of care and have consistent access to food and clean water. This depicts practices all the way down to transporting, handling, and slaughtering the animal.

LOW SODIUM

Sodium is a mineral found in foods and can also be added to foods. Nutritionally, sodium helps balance normal fluid within the body. When it comes to minerals, we're looking for balance — we don't want to use iodized salt, as it contains only two minerals and can create imbalance in the body. Use least-processed Celtic sea salt or Redmond's pink salt to keep your minerals and thus sodium in balance.

SUGAR-FREE

Sugar-free means there is no added sugar within the product. This term does not include artificial sweeteners — in fact, these products are often sweetened with artificial sweeteners.

PLANT-BASED

Plant based is most often used to denote avoiding foods that contain any type of animal product. Most labels have this to indicate that the food is derived from plants or other non animal components. When it comes to non-animal based meats, you'll often see lots of soy, chemicals, additives and thickeners.

LOW CALORIE

Low calorie refers to a restriction of calories contained in the food. Foods can still be nutritionally disproportionate — high fat or high carb, for example. Remember, a calorie is a unit of energy. Each type of macronutrient in food (fat, protein, or carbohydrate) provides energy to the body to be able to function. We need calories/energy in every cell of our body. Naturally low-calorie foods are fruits and vegetables.

LOW FAT

Fats help absorb fat soluble vitamins like vitamins A, D, E, and K — we need them! Fats also helps improve the taste of our food and increases satiety or fullness. Fats provide high caloric energy, help build our cell membranes and act as a protective lining for our organs in the body!

Our hormones are also derived from healthy fats — they're the first move for fixing hormone balance via food. Let's stick with healthy fats like avocados, pastured animal fats, coconut oil, and olive oils.

Canola, vegetable and soy oils are toxic to our bodies. Animal fats from inferior animals can be toxic as well — mammals store toxins in the fat tissue, making a pastured and/or organic animal raised with the least amount of toxicity very important when buying animal fats.

SPECIAL DIETS

KETOGENIC (KETO)

The Ketogenic (Keto) diet emphasizes a high fat, low carbohydrate way of eating. The primary energy source for the body is fat, not carbohydrates. The Keto diet focuses on consuming healthy fat, protein, and vegetables, while restricting most carbohydrates such as starches, grains, honey, fruit, and beans. The Keto diet was originally implemented to reduce seizures in children with epilepsy.

A therapeutic Keto diet has many neurological benefits, such as reducing inflammation in the brain. Research has also shown the Keto diet to be beneficial in improving autism symptoms. In addition, those with metabolic conditions, neurological disorders, and seizures can see benefits from a Keto diet. I love to work Keto components in the diet of those looking to heal blood sugar dysregulation like Type 2 Diabetes or pre-diabetes.

WESTON A. PRICE DIET

Weston A. Price was a dentist who researched the connection between nutrition and health in indigenous cultures around the world. He used their dental health as an indicator of the effects nutrition had on their overall health. Because of the effects he observed of modern nutrition on dental health (cavities, jaw structure, nasal shape), he developed a set of dietary principles that support a return to a traditional, cultural way of eating.

These principles incorporate pasture-raised and Grass-fed animal foods and fats, unsaturated and saturated fats, raw milk and other dairy products, soaked and sprouted grains, nuts and seeds, bone broths, fermented foods, and avoid processed foods, additives, refined flour, processed flour and oils, and soy products.

The principles of the Weston A. Price diet would be beneficial for just about everyone to implement. In particular children and adults with ADHD, autism, and other neurological disorders will benefit from the Weston A. Price diet due to its anti-inflammatory properties and avoidance of processed foods and additives.

PALEO

The goal of the Paleo diet is to increase foods that heal and nourish the body, while removing foods that promote disease and inflammation. The Paleo diet provides a balance of nutrients while avoiding refined foods and empty calories. Paleo is a whole-food and nutrient-dense focused way of eating.

The Paleo (Paleolithic) Diet focuses on foods that our ancestors ate such as meat, vegetables, fruits, eggs, nuts, and seeds. The Paleo Diet avoids grains, beans, dairy, refined sugars, and processed foods as those were not available to our ancestors as hunter gatherers.

The purpose of the Paleo Diet is to avoid modern foods that contribute to modern health issues such as inflammation, pain, digestive issues, blood sugar dysfunction, neurological conditions, behavioral disorders, learning disabilities, and obesity.

Following a Paleo diet there are plenty of nutrient-dense foods to choose from including:

- All meats
- All seafood
- Eggs
- Vegetables
- Fruits
- Edible fungi (i.e. mushrooms)
- Nuts and seeds
- Herbs and spices
- Unrefined, unprocessed fats from animals and plants
- Probiotic and fermented foods

Paleo removes:

- Processed food and additives
- Gluten and grains
- Legumes and soy
- Dairy
- Refined Sugar
- Seed and refined oils
- Excessive Alcohol

The Paleo Diet is where I suggest most people begin. The term has become popular, recipes are easy to google for and lots can be done with the ingredients available: loads of healing, too. Children with ADHD, autism, neurological conditions, immune disorders, metabolic conditions, and digestive dysfunction often have inflammation and oxidative stress.

Foods incorporated in the Paleo Diet are nutrient dense and contain minerals, fat soluble vitamins, fatty acids, and amino acids that help replenish nutrient deficiencies, support the microbiome, and provide the building blocks needed to grow and heal.

LOW FODMAP DIET

FODMAPs are different fermentable carbohydrates. When implementing, a Low FODMAP diet is initially restrictive and later incorporates individual foods, systematically, to determine tolerance. These fermentable carbohydrates feed both beneficial and pathogenic bacteria.

The pathogenic bacteria ferment the carbohydrates and this creates gas. These carbohydrates are also osmotic meaning they draw water into the colon and can cause diarrhea for some.

Restricted foods include certain fruits with high fructose like apples, pears and mango, high fructose corn syrup, lactose-containing dairy products, fructans such as onions, garlic, inulin, and wheat, galacto-oligosaccharide rich foods including beans and legumes, as well as foods with polyols like avocados and prunes.

Fodmap stands for fermentable oligo—, di—, and monosaccharides and polyols.

- Oligosaccharides: wheat, rye, nuts, legumes, artichokes, garlic, and onion
- Disaccharides: products which contact lactose such as milk, yogurt, soft cheese, ice cream, buttermilk, condensed milk, and whipped cream
- Monosaccharides: foods which contain fructose, such as apples, pears, watermelon, and mango and sweeteners such as honey, agave nectar, and high fructose corn syrup
- Polyols: mannitol, sorbitol, xylitol and isomalt

Most reactions to FODMAPs occur in the gastrointestinal tract. A Low FODMAPs diet is used when these fermentable carbohydrates are suspected to be causing gas, pain, and digestive irregularity, and other digestive symptoms.

This diet can also be helpful in cases of SIBO and additional microbiome issues. Common symptoms a Low FODMAP diet can address include diarrhea, constipation, gas, bloating, gastrointestinal pain, and an increase in any symptoms affected by pain, microbiome, or other gut state, and SIBO symptoms. The Low FODMAP diet, like many others, is a tool, for a time. If you find yourself only functional on a Low FODMAP diet, please work with a practitioner to find the root cause of your distress.

SPECIFIC CARBOHYDRATE DIET (SCD) AND GAPS DIET

These diets involve removing all starches (polysaccharides) and complex sugars (disaccharides). Simple sugar (monosaccharide) carbohydrates found in honey, natural fruit sugar, and non-starchy vegetables are allowed.

The goal is to reduce gut inflammation and promote healing by "starving out" pathogenic gut bacteria as the sugars and starches that feed them are eliminated. These disaccharides and polysaccharides require carbohydrate digesting enzymes.

When these enzymes are not present or are not performing appropriately due to dysfunction, the carbohydrates remain in the gastrointestinal tract undigested and become food for the microbes and pathogens.

Studies have shown that some children with autism lack these digestive enzymes and have digestive systems that are overrun with pathogenic bacteria and yeast.

Foods that are avoided include maple syrup, cane sugar, agave nectar, brown rice syrup, and other sources of sugars, all starches including grains, corn, potatoes, and sweet potatoes. Additionally foods that contain these ingredients including most baked goods, candy, jelly, fruit snacks, granola bars, juices, fruit punch style drinks, ice cream, soda, chocolate milk, cereal, and other pre-packaged and freezer foods that contain sugar in their ingredient list are also avoided.

The goal of these diets are to improve gastrointestinal issues for people dealing with diagnoses such as Autism, Crohn's disease, ulcerative colitis, celiac disease, diverticulitis, cystic fibrosis, and chronic diarrhea. More focus is given to increasing pre-digested, nourishing and nutrient-dense foods. While I like SCD or GAPS for a lengthy healing period, if symptoms aren't resolving, please work with a practitioner who utilizes testing to find the root cause of dysfunction.

GLUTEN-FREE, CASEIN-FREE (GFCF)

Gluten is a family of proteins that are found in grains such as wheat, rye, spelt, and barley. The two main proteins are glutenin and gliadin, with gliadin being the protein that typically causes adverse health reactions.

Casein is a complete protein that is found in dairy products. All mammals produce casein as a component in their milk for their offspring. Casein contains all essential amino acids, and due to its structure, is a slow-digesting protein.

Casein can contribute to adverse health reactions in those with a dairy sensitivity. This diet can be supportive for those with any gluten or dairy allergy, intolerance, or sensitivity. Because of the high reactivity that both gluten and dairy can have for some, this diet can also be beneficial for those with symptoms of, or diagnosed autism and digestive dysfunction (such as IBS).

GLUTEN FREE, CASEIN FREE, & SOY FREE (GFCFSF)

Gluten is a family of proteins that are found in grains such as wheat, rye, spelt, and barley. The two main proteins are glutenin and gliadin, with gliadin being the protein that typically causes adverse health reactions. Casein is a complete protein that is found in dairy products.

All mammals produce casein as a component in their milk for their offspring. Casein contains all essential amino acids, and due to its structure, is a slow-digesting protein. Casein can contribute to adverse health reactions in those with a dairy sensitivity.

Soy is a meat-free protein source. Soybeans contain all essential amino acids making it a complete protein source. Soy contains a high concentration of phytoestrogens that are similar in function to human estrogen. These can bind to estrogen receptors in the human body and can cause weak or anti-estrogenic activity.

Soy also has a similar protein structure as gluten and casein, so it can cause similar issues. Lastly, soy is one of the most genetically modified crops and should be avoided. This therapeutic diet is immensely healing for those with autism and gut-brain diagnoses like ADD, ADHD, OCD, depression and anxiety. Also helpful for those with stomachaches, diarrhea and

constipation, congestion and sleep apnea, headaches, and picky eating.

LOW OXALATE DIET

Oxalates are protective molecules found in plants that have a number of functions, such as protection from bugs eating them. In the human body oxalates bind to calcium, magnesium, zinc, and iron. This can create oxalate calcium kidney stones.

Oxalates can cause oxidative stress in the body, impair cellular energy, disrupt the microbiome, and deplete minerals and vitamins. The effects of this can cause a variety of symptoms such as fatigue, weakness, loss of muscle tone, gas and bloating, burning feet, frequent urination, urinary pain, brain fog, anxiety and depression, moodiness, blood sugar dysfunction, thyroid disruption, and kidney stones.

High oxalate issues can show up on certain laboratory markers. A low oxalate diet should be implemented slowly and over time. Foods high in oxalates include spinach, swiss chard, beet greens, beets, sweet potatoes, potatoes, rhubarb, nuts, some seeds, legumes, certain grains, some fruits, and chocolate.

Oxalates have been linked to autism, autoimmune disorders, and chronic disease. Children and adults with various immune, neurological, and digestive issues can benefit from a low oxalate diet.

FEINGOLD/LOW PHENOL DIET

This diet removes artificial food additives and foods high in salicylates. Some children have difficulty processing salicylates (phenol) and this can lead to a build up in the body. Salicylate or phenol backup can have negative effects on the brain and lead to behavioral and physical symptoms listed below.

High salicylate foods are apples, grapes, berries, honey, almonds, peanuts, oranges, apricots, cherries, ketchup, chili powder, cider and cider vinegar, cocoa, cloves, coffee, cucumbers, pickles, currants, red grapes, raisins, plums, prunes, tangerines, tea, tomatoes, wine and wine vinegar, oil of wintergreen, and most herbs/spices. Food additives such as artificial colors, food dyes, artificial flavoring and fragrances, preservatives such as BHA, BHT, TBHQ, and artificial sweeteners are also removed.

Many adults with ADHD, autism, neurological and immune system disorders, and phenol sensitivity find healing with this diet.

Common symptoms of phenol sensitivity in children includes dark circles under the eyes, redness on the cheeks and ears, ear infections, asthma, sinus problems, diarrhea, hyperactivity, impulsivity, aggression, headache, head banging/self-injury, impatience, short attention span, difficulty falling asleep, night walking for several hours, inappropriate laughter, hives, stomach aches, bed wetting and day wetting, dyslexia, sensitivity to noise/lights/touch, speech difficulties, tics, and some forms of seizures.

LOW SALICYLATE, AMINE, AND GLUTAMATE (LOW SAG)

These are all food chemicals that react similarly in the body. Salicylates are found in plants/plant foods, artificial colors, flavors, and preservatives. Amines are found in a variety of foods including meat, fish, fruits, and vegetables at varying levels.

Glutamate is found in fermented and cured foods. This diet removes salicylates, amines, and glutamates that are overwhelming certain people's systems and contributing to symptoms.

In certain indivudals, these naturally occurring food chemicals can be difficult to detoxify due to poor sulfation. By removing them from the diet it decreases the burden on the body to restore the microbiome and other systems affected to improve food tolerances.

Conditions associated with poor sulfation include ADHD, autism, autoimmune conditions such as Lupus, and microbiome disruption will benefit from this therapeutic diet. Common symptoms that can be supported with a low SAG diet include hyperactivity, redness on the cheeks and ears, irritability, defiant behavior, self injury, aggression, sleeping issues such as night waking or terrors, skin rashes, respiratory issues, diarrhea, crying easily, bedwetting, urinary urgency, incontinence.

ANTIFUNGAL OR ANTI CANDIDA DIET

The anti-Candida diet promotes a low-sugar, anti-inflammatory style of eating that focuses on improving gut health and eliminates the sugars that feed Candida overgrowth. The diet is high in non-starchy vegetables, some low-sugar fruits, gluten-free grains, some dairy products, and fermented foods. Improving gut health, and restoring the balance of the bacteria and yeast in the body is the goal of the anti-Candida diet.

This can help to relieve symptoms from Candida-overgrowth such as bloating, indigestion, yeast infections, fatigue, nausea, diarrhea, and gas. Candida is a species of yeast that lives in the gut. Typically, it co-exists with the rest of the microbiome; however, it can grow out of control under the right circumstances.

Other bacteria in the gut usually keep Candida

check, but different factors can affect this, such as a high-sugar diet, a course of antibiotics, or chronic stress. There are many symptoms of Candida overgrowth including fatigue, brain fog, digestive issues, sinus infections, food allergies, yeast infections, mild depression, joint pain, and much more. Symptoms can vary person to person depending on the overall health of one's gut.

The health of the gut is linked to the immune system, blood sugar regulation, heart health, and digestion. If you have been following me for a while, then you know that gut health also impacts mental health. An unhealthy gut can cause problems throughout every part of the body.

The anti-Candida diet is for those experiencing any of the above symptoms of Candida overgrowth. If you want more confirmation of whether or not you have a Candida overgrowth, this can be detected with a GI Map stool test or by working with a practitioner to take a candida symptom quiz. Candida has become a buzzword, something we quickly self-diagnose - testing or a strong symptom load are adequate to support fungal healing.

BODY ECOLOGY DIET

The Body Ecology diet focuses on improving the ecology of the body with beneficial microbes. The Body Ecology Diet incorporates cultured and fermented foods, meat, fish, eggs, vegetables (land and sea), sour fruit, some seeds, natural fats/oils. It avoids legumes, unfermented dairy, sweet fruits, starchy vegetables, nuts, all except four grains (amaranth, buckwheat, quinoa and millet), and refined oils and sugars.

The purpose of this diet is to supply the body with microbes and nutrient dense foods to feed the microbiome and support the digestive system. The Body Ecology Diet is used to support overall health, starting with the gut.

The Body Ecology Diet can be useful for those with symptoms of digestive issues, candida/yeast/fungal infections, after taking antibiotics to rebuild the gut microbiome, weak immune function, reactions to gluten, dairy or soy, food allergies or environmental sensitivities.

For those with neurological challenges that have underlying dysbiosis, such as with depression or autism, The Body Ecology Diet can be used to support gut health and clean up the diet. This is a more "loose" gut healing diet, though not too popular, so recipes are hard to come by.

LOW HISTAMINE DIET

Histamine is a compound that's found in the cells of our body and also naturally occurs in some foods. Histamine plays a role in inflammation by providing an immediate response to inflammatory events and is also an important part of the immune system.

Histamine also regulates gastric acid secretion needed for digestion, and aids the body in delivering blood, nutrients, and oxygen to various parts of the body.

Histamine is typically broken down by the DAO and HNMT enzymes. For someone with a histamine intolerance these enzymes are impaired and histamine builds up in the body.

Other causes of histamine intolerance include environmental triggers such as dust mites and pollen, excessive alcohol, a diet high in fermented foods, protein, and aged foods, excess estrogen, adrenal dysfunction, too little sleep, stress, nutrient deficiencies, and gut dysfunction.

Histamine intolerance does not have a specific test to diagnose. However, histamine and DAO enzyme levels can be measured through blood and urine screenings. Common symptoms of histamine intolerance include headaches, migraines, diarrhea, eczema, low blood pressure, runny nose, heartburn, PMS, seasonal allergies, food allergies, asthma, motion sickness, nausea, vomiting, irritability, and loose stools.

Diet is an important part of determining if one is suffering from histamine intolerance and then managing it. A low histamine diet is implemented by eliminating histamine-rich foods and seeing if symptoms begin to clear up.

In addition to a low histamine diet, underlying conditions such as digestive dysfunction (IBS, SIBO, Celiac disease) must also be addressed, so it is important to work with a practitioner to take an integrative approach to the root cause. Layering this diet in is my third most used and effective diet after Paleo and GFDFSF.

VEGAN AND RAW FOOD DIETS

A vegan diet consists only of eating plants and plant-based alternatives to animal products. A vegan diet is composed of lots of fruits and vegetables, legumes such as beans, peas, and lentils, nuts and seeds, grains, vegetable oils, and dairy alternatives such as soy, coconut, and almond products.

A raw food diet is similar to a vegan diet with an emphasis on many plant foods. A raw food diet goes further in that it focuses on uncooked and unprocessed foods. A raw food diet can consist of animal products such as raw eggs, meat, and fish, and unpasteurized dairy products.

I don't recommend either of these diets to clients for the important reasons that both of these diets are nutrient deficient and do not promote a balanced diet. Common nutrient deficiencies include calcium, iron, zinc, vitamin D, B12, and omega-3 fatty acids. In addition, many plant-based alternatives on the market are loaded with hydrogenated oils (canola, sunflower, safflower) and additives like guar gum and carrageenan.

Animal protein far surpasses plant-based protein options in nutrient density and is needed for hormone

balance and blood sugar regulation.

FOOD SENSITIVITY DIET

The purpose of a food sensitivity diet is to remove inflammatory foods that may be causing adverse health reactions. The top inflammatory foods are gluten, casein, soy, corn, eggs, citrus, peanuts, chocolate, and sugar.

By removing these foods, inflammation in the gut and the rest of the body can be reduced and eliminated completely. In addition, a food sensitivity test (I prefer the MRT-170) can be run to determine specific sensitivities. Those foods are also removed to allow the body to uninflame and promote healing. After a period of several weeks, these foods can slowly be reintroduced to determine tolerance.

Inflammation is at the root of most chronic diseases. This is especially true for neurological conditions such as anxiety, depression, ADHD, and autism. This diet can be very helpful when a gluten free, dairy free diet has not produced satisfactory results or during an intensive digestive healing phase.

An MRT food sensitivity test takes the guesswork out of figuring out what foods one is sensitive to and allows for deep healing during a strategic healing season using other tests like the GI-MAP Stool Test or Organic Acids Test.

AUTOIMMUNE PROTOCOL DIET

The AIP (Autoimmune Protocol) Diet is implemented to reduce inflammation, pain, and other symptoms that are caused by autoimmune diseases. For those with an autoimmune disease, the body produces antibodies that attack healthy cells and tissues, rather than fight infections. There are certain foods that increase inflammation and the likelihood of leaky gut. When leaky gut is occurring in the body, an immune response is elicited to fight the food particles that escaped the small intestine and are now in the bloodstream. For an individual with an autoimmune disease, the body may not be able to respond appropriately due to their already compromised immune system. The AIP diet focuses on eliminating these foods and replacing them with nutrient-dense options to promote health, help heal leaky gut, reduce inflammation, and reduce symptoms of the autoimmune disease.

This diet can be helpful to those with an autoimmune disease such as Celiac disease, IBS/IBD, Lupus, Rheumatoid arthritis, Type 1 diabetes, and Psoriasis. The AIP diet can help reduce common symptoms that are caused by autoimmune disease including joint pain, fatigue, abdominal pain, tissue and nerve damage, fatigue, and brain fog. While the AIP diet is very helpful, I do not recommend staying on it long term without digging for the root cause with the help of a practitioner.

GLUTEN FAQ

WHAT IS GLUTEN?

Gluten is a protein that is found in several grains. Small but mighty, gluten makes up only about 9-10% of the grain kernel. The gluten protein contains two parts, one part contributes to the elasticity of a gluten-containing product, and the other part the extensibility. Gluten is what makes bread dough stretchy and elastic!

It is important to check labels of packaged products for any of these grains if you are avoiding gluten! You can also look for the regulated "GF" logo to give you an "easy button" for certified 100% Gluten Free products.

IS GLUTEN BAD?

While I wouldn't label gluten as "bad" it is a contributor to inflammation in many people, some more so than others, and slowly contributes to "leaky gut" or intestinal permeability in all people because of its interaction in the small intestine.

WHAT CAN GLUTEN REACTIVITY LOOK LIKE?

Intolerance: Symptoms of gluten intolerance include GI distress such as diarrhea, bloating, and gas. While there is no specific test to conclusively diagnose an intolerance, increased inflammation can be checked with a GI-Map Stool Test. Symptoms are substantial enough an indicator that a person would be better off avoiding gluten.

Allergy: A true allergy is a severe immune response. An allergy can produce symptoms such as hives, itching, swelling, and in severe cases, anaphylaxis. A true allergen should be avoided.

Celiac Disease: Around 1% of the population is affected by Celiac disease. Celiac disease is an autoimmune condition that causes intestinal damage at gluten exposure. This affects the body's ability to absorb and assimilate nutrients. Those with Celiac disease should take strict measures to eliminate gluten.

Thyroid Conditions: While gluten consumption is not a cause of hypothyroid conditions or Hashimoto's Thyroiditis autoimmune disease, it is an inflammatory product that can trigger an immune response.

This contributes to inflammation in the body, including the thyroid, whose molecular structure is very similar to gluten — this similarity can provoke the immune system to attack the thyroid tissue = thyroid autoimmunity. In addition, gluten can cause GI distress which impacts the body's ability to absorb nutrients vital to the health of the thyroid.

BUT WHAT ABOUT SOURDOUGH?

There are some gluten containing products that those with an intolerance or sensitivity may be able to tolerate. These include ancient grains and sourdough. Ancient grains are less processed than the typical wheat.

The gluten in sourdough has been fermented making it easier to digest and less inflammatory. When working to heal the gut 100% gluten-free is the way to be. Sourdough may cause less reactivity, but the damages caused to the small intestine and immune activation from exposure take 3-6 months to heal.

Remember, that sourdough did have healthy bacteria in the starter that does the fermentation work, but is of no microbial benefit to the gut after cooking. Sourdough still contains wheat and gluten with no added probiotics.

AREN'T CHEMICALS GLUTEN'S PROBLEM?

Wheat crops today are heavily contaminated by chemicals and pesticides. In addition, some have been genetically modified to withstand pests and the elements. These GMO, chemically sprayed crops may be a reason for the rise in gluten intolerance seen today.

Most grain crops in the US are exposed to glyphosate or Round-Up. This chemical is a low-grade antibiotic and one we want to avoid at all costs, as it slowly acts on our good and bad bacteria in the gut, killing them, just as it does when sprayed on plants to kill pests.

WHAT CONTAINS GLUTEN?

Wheat
Rye
Barley
Spelt
Durum
Semolina
Farro
Triticale
Kamut
Commercial Oats
Semolina
Hydrolyzed Vegetable Protein
Dextrin
MSG
Soy Sauce
(unless wheat-free like Tamari)
Potato chips/fries
(unless gluten-free, many are not)
Malt
Citric Acid
Sauces and Gravies
Some Bologna and Hot Dogs
Artificial flavors and coloring
"Spices" and Some Spice Blends

GLUTEN-FREE GRAINS AND FOODS:

Quinoa
Buckwheat
Millet
Amaranth
Gluten-Free Oats
Brown and white rice
Wild rice
Corn
Sorghum
Tapioca
Nut Flours
Seed Flours
Coconut Flour
Bean Flours
Yucca and Cassava flours
Gelatin
Xanthan Gum
Arrowroot
Guar Gum
Agar

LABEL READING AND THE
GREAT PANTRY CLEANOUT

If you're in the early days of transitioning to a new way of eating, just know that it will only be new for a short time. You will adjust, it will feel normal and it won't feel overwhelming. Best encouragement for the transition? Imagine how good it'll feel when you (or your littles) can open the fridge and pantry and see only nourishing food options.

I recommend going through and tossing out all of the things that no longer nourish your body, but make sure you hit up the grocery store or have a delivery scheduled full of things to help you not feel deprived. Find things you are excited to try.

Explore buying clubs like Sam's Club, Costco and Thrive Market. Wander through inspiring farmer's markets or sign up for your local Community Supported Agriculture (CSA) subscription.

MY BEST TIPS FOR LABEL READING:

1. Ingredients are listed in order of most-used to least-used in a product. If a chemical, gum or sweetener is listed early in a label, I tend to avoid more than if it's listed later, suggesting a lesser amount.
2. If you cannot pronounce a word, it's likely a chemical or additive: pass on those.
3. Learn to look for the names of refined sugars. While you can rely on the carbohydrate and sugars values in the nutrition facts, learning to identify when a product uses more than one sugar is key.
4. Allergen info is included on most all labels and is your "easy button". The label will say something like **CONTAINS: WHEAT, SOY AND TREE NUTS.** If these are foods you're avoiding, this is a simple "no" label. The allergen list takes a bit of know-how as gluten isn't listed, though wheat contains gluten, so this would make a label containing wheat a "no" label for those eating gluten-free.
5. Net carbs are a helpful gauge. To get a feel for how fiber is effecting the carbohydrate count, subtract the dietary fiber (grams) from the total carbohydrate (grams) quantities and you can quickly identify a food that is more likely to spike blood sugar (higher number) or is less likely to spike blood sugar thanks to the added fiber (lower number).

A WORD ON FORTIFIED FOODS AND ADDITIVES

Fortified foods and food additives are as plentiful as rain in spring. My easy rule – if it was a mother or could be grown by a mother, then we eat it. Otherwise, we don't.

You'll want to stay away from heavily processed foods, especially when they contain artificial flavors and dyes. These substances and chemicals are often artificial or unnatural and are seen by the body as toxins. They will need to be detoxified and offer no nutritional value.

Additionally, since the 1960's, foods have been fortified as an effort to replace missing nutrients and offer nutrients to those who may have limited access to foods and focus on consuming processed foods like cereals, breads, canned items etc.

These fortified vitamins and minerals added to foods are synthetic, often stimulating neurological issues, impairing or placing a great burden on detox or plain causing digestive or allergic reactions in some.

I would encourage you to avoid all these sorts of additives and chemicals in not only your foods, but your personal care and home products. The less toxins entering the body through the skin, breath or food, the more your body will focus on building health and healing over repair and extra detoxification.

To work on detoxifying all avenues of your life: beauty, body care, personal care and more visit www.heyheymae.com/detoxyourlife for my current suggestions.

NAMES OF REFINED SUGARS AND WHY THEY MATTER

Refined sugar can go by many names on ingredient labels, and food companies will use more than one type of refined sugar to disguise the fact that — in essence — sugar can be the largest single ingredient in a given food item. Overall, we want to continually limit the amount of sugar we take in, aiming for next to none. We will still consume sugars naturally through fruits, carby veggies, grains and more — who needs extra synthetic sugars? Not us.

INGREDIENTS TO AVOID

All food colorings (Red #40, Yellow #40, Red #4, Blue #1 etc.)

Aspartame

Benzoic Acid

BHA

BHT

Calcium Caseinate or Sodium Caseinate

Caramel Color

Dextrose

Equal

Folic Acid

High Fructose Corn Syrup

Hydrogenated Fats

MSG

Oxybenzone

Nitrates/Nitrites

Nutrasweet

Parabens (methyl—, isobutyl—, propyl— and others)

Phthalates (DBP, DEHP, DEP and others)

Polyethylene glycol (PEG compounds)

Polysorbate 80

Propionic Acid

Trisodium Phosphate

Reduced Iron

Saccharine

Sodium Lauryl Sulfate and Sodium Laureth Sulfate (SLS and SLES)

Sorbic Acid

Soy Lecithin

Sucralose

Sulfites

Splenda

Sweet N'Low

TBHQ

Textured Protein

Vitamin A Palmitate

Yeast Nutrient, Yeast Extract, Yeast Food and Autolyzed Yeast

REFINED SUGARS

Barley malt

Beet sugar

Brown sugar

Buttered syrup

Cane juice crystals

Cane juice solids

Cane juice

Cane sugar

Caramel syrup

Carob syrup

Concentrated fruit juice

Corn syrup

Corn syrup solids

Date sugar

Dehydrated cane juice

Dehydrated fruit juice

Dextran

Dextrin

Dextrose

Diastase

Diastatic malt

Disaccharides

Ethyl maltol

Fructose

Fruit juice crystals

Fruit puree

Galactose

Glucose

Glucose-fructose

Glucose solids

Golden syrup

High-fructose corn syrup

Honey

Invert sugar

Lactose

Malt

Malt extract

Malt syrup

Maltodextrin

Maltose

Maple syrup

Molasses

Polysaccharides

Raw sugar

Refiner's syrup

Rice extract

Rice syrup

Sorghum syrup

Sucanat

Sucrose

Sugar

Tapioca syrup

Turbinado

Yellow sugar

HEALTHY FATS 101:
FAT AND OILS GUIDE

One of the most confusing nutrition spaces for my clients are fats. You, too? Many of us grew up amidst the low-fat, no-fat craze, perpetuated by booming seed and vegetable oil production in America.

Quality animal fats were vilified. Your favorite corner dollar burger shop swapped out beef tallow in the frier for more affordable, health-damaging canola-soy blend frying oil. So sad.

Now many of us are confused as to whether we need fats, should live on them like the ketogenic diet suggests, or plain avoid them all together because Aunt B once said that fats'll make ya fat! My take? Healthy fats are where it's at: for weight loss, blood sugar regulation, hormone balance, lovely skin and more.

WHY DO WE NEED HEALTHY FATS?

Fats have many different roles in the body including:

- Fats are required to make the structure of every cell in our body: each cell membrane is made of lipids.

- Fats are needed to make your sex hormones: estrogen, progesterone, testosterone.

- Fats are essential for proper liver function: did you know cholesterol is a lipid or fat, that we both eat and produce cholesterol in the body?

- Fats are needed to make bile, bile is essential for the digestion of fats and the elimination of toxins. Think of bile as your intestinal sanitizer.

- Fats must be present in food for us to absorb those fat-soluble vitamins A, D, E, and K.

- Fats provide stable energy. Think strong and steady with no energy crashes.

- Fat is fuel for the brain, fat also helps nourish rapidly growing littles' brains.

- Fat is needed to strengthen the gut lining to avoid

WHICH FATS ARE BEST TO CONSUME?

Almonds	Macadamia nuts
Avocado oil	MCT oil
Bacon (nitrate-free)	Nut Butters
Grass-fed beef	Olive oil
Grass-fed bison	Pecans
Grass-fed lamb	Pumpkin seeds
Brazil nuts	Wild-caught salmon
Grass-fed butter	Sardines
Cashews	Sesame seeds
Coconut oil	Sunflower seeds
Dark Chocolate	Tahini
Duck Fat	Tallow
Pasture-raised eggs	Walnuts
Ghee	

intestinal permeability or "leaky gut". Fats can also act as a healing agent for leaky gut.

- Fats slow the absorption of food, helping to regulate appetite, signal fullness hormones and stabilize blood glucose levels.

- Fats are required for the body to heal — they promote both inflammation and anti-inflammation.

- Fats make foods taste better, providing satiation. Have you ever had a baked french fry, followed by one fried in oil? Enough said.

TYPES OF FATS TO CONSUME:

- **Saturated Fats:** coconut oil, Grass-fed meats, eggs, goose fat, ghee, butter, and dairy.

- **Monounsaturated Fats:** olive oil, avocados, avocado oil, lard, and poultry.

- **Polyunsaturated Fats:** wild-caught fish, fish oils, and flaxseed

TIP: Rotate them! With all food, we were made to have variety! Healthy, pastured animal fats offer us Vitamin D, while coconut offers antibacterial and antifungal properties, still avocados pack a big Vitamin E punch — see — we need all the fats! Stick to those whole forms here, too. Your body is less likely to get an imbalanced fatty acid profile when we eat whole-foods and yet, some seasons require supplemental fats. I love polyunsatured fats in whole-food rotation in the diet — eat the fish > rely on a bottle of Kirkland fish oils or tub of almonds for all your omegas.

Fats are like people — it takes all kinds, except for the toxic ones!

FATS TO AVOID:

Trans fats, hydrogenated oils and processed seed oils like canola, soy, sunflower and safflower. These oils are very inflammatory and can raise "bad" LDL cholesterol levels and triglycerides, while lowering HDL "good" cholesterol. They're also much less stable and seen by the body as a toxin, not a tool for building health. The body sees these fats as another substance that must be eliminated.

When we remove these fats from our diets, we see our symptom load decrease as toxicity decreases, the body's inflammatory load shifts and our liver, gallbladder health increases.

Still struggling with fat digestion or looking to focus your healing on fatty acid function? Let's look at therapeutic foods to help.

THERAPEUTIC FOODS TO SUPPORT FATTY ACID FUNCTION:

Artichoke: Increases bile production, which is necessary for the breakdown and absorption of fats. I love artichokes steamed and canned whole artichokes and artichoke hearts in water. Make my breakfast casserole for a yummy intro to artichokes.

Almonds and almond oil: Contain healthy unsaturated fatty acids along with vitamin E, copper, and magnesium. Easy to go overboard on, with the nut

butter and nut flour focus of late.

Avocado Oil: Helps process food more efficiently and improves digestion. Contains high levels of monounsaturated fatty acids that help absorb fat soluble vitamins. A wonderful substitute in baking, thanks to its stability up, above 500°F.

Beets: High levels of folate and manganese support gallbladder function. Grate and mix with green apple and/or carrot (drizzle with olive oil and lemon juice or apple cider vinegar) and eat as a condiment. I'm also a big fan of my beet recipe options, two ways.

Butter: An antioxidant, full of nourishment for the colon, butter can reduce potential intestinal conditions, and increases the effectiveness of absorbing nutrients. We always want quality butter, choose butter from pastured or Grass-fed animals when possible.

Coconut Oil: Coconut oil is absorbed and digested quickly with little to no effort. This medium-chain fatty acid is broken down almost immediately when coming in contact with the enzymes in saliva. Available in a always-liquid version called "fractionated" coconut oil.

Cod Liver Oil: High levels of Vitamins A, D, and E. One of my favorite fats for supporting language development in children, gut healing and overall brain development.

Dandelion: A digestion powerhouse, dandelion enhances the flow of bile, improves liver congestion, bile duct inflammation, hepatitis, gallstones, and jaundice. Dandelion has a direct effect on the liver, raising bile production and flow to the gallbladder, and stimulating the contraction and release of stored bile. Available as a tea as well as greens you can enjoy in salads or cooked — the tea is a morning staple for many.

Duck/Chicken/Goose/Turkey Fat: Poultry fat's medium chain fatty acids are a source of an antimicrobial fatty acid. Duck fat is my favorite poultry fat to cook with followed closely by the chicken fat that rises to the top of the pot when making chicken stock.

Flaxseed Oil: High in ALA Omega-6 fatty acids and can help with improving gallstones. Improves gut health and aides in weight loss. Don't go overboard, here.

Lard: A monounsaturated fat that is a stable fat, helps the body absorb Vitamin D, and is lower in Omega-6 fatty acids. Lard is natural and does not go through a hydrogenation process. Source from your local farmer.

Lemons: High in Vitamin C and fiber. Helps thin bile and enhances overall digestion. Bile health is why a morning lemon water is credited as a morning detox method.

Olive Oil: A delicate oil that should not be used for cooking at high heat. Olive oil is a healthy monounsaturated fat, containing a large amount of antioxidants and has strong anti-inflammatory properties. A quick drizzle is a great way to add fats to a meal otherwise lacking them.

Palm Kernel Oil: Made from kernels of palm fruits and has a similar composition to coconut oil. Rich in antioxidants, Vitamins K and A. On occasion, I use palm oil where shortening would be used in baking.

Radishes: Another fat digesting aid, the sulfur-based chemicals in radishes increase the flow of bile, helping to maintain a healthy gallbladder and liver function. Rich source of B vitamins, calcium, magnesium, copper, and many other minerals. Slice thin on a mandolin and enjoy crispy slices when refrigerated in a bit of water.

Tallow: Stable and ideal for cooking at high temperatures, beef tallow is a great option when frying.

FOOD QUALITY: BUYING QUALITY PROTEINS AND BONES

GRASS-FED VS. PASTURE-RAISED

When ruminant animals like beef, lamb, buffalo, bison, and goat are labeled "Grass-fed," it means that they have been fed grass for at least some of their lives. This is in stark contrast to animals raised exclusively on feedlots, where they are raised on corn, grains, and commercial feed.

That said, the term is not tightly regulated, and even "Grass-fed" animals can actually be finished on grains for the last few months before they come to market.

To ensure that an animal has only eaten grass as nature intended, look for meats labeled "Grass-fed, Grass-finished" or "100% Grass-fed." This is important because animals fed exclusively grass live healthier lives and produce healthier food. 100% Grass-fed beef,

for example, has a much more favorable ratio of Omega-6 to Omega-3 fatty acids than those raised on corn, grains, etc.

This ratio of fatty acids is very important to our cellular health and is found more favorably present in Grass-fed and pastured animals.

"Pasture-raised" or "pastured" animals spend most of their time outside, meaning they have access to their natural diets: grass for cows, insects for chickens, etc. But some pasture-raised animals may be fed grains, too, especially in the winter when the pasture is covered with snow. Keep looking for "100% Grass-fed". Pigs and chickens, for example, need grain to thrive.

The key here is that pasture-raised refers more to where an animal eats, while Grass-fed refers to what. Want to know exactly how your food was raised and what they ate? Your best bet is to get to know your local farmers or ranchers. It creates a more visceral connection with your food, shows respect for those who grow it, and allows you to ask questions directly.

When shopping for bones to make nourishing bone broth, an organic, pastured animal is your best

choice. The same is true when looking for animal fats. Remember that animals, like humans, store toxins in their fat cells, therefore we want the healthiest animal possible when shopping for fats. Organic, wild and pastured are your top terms to look for.

CAGE-FREE VS. FREE-RANGE POULTRY & EGGS

You will often see poultry and eggs labeled as "cage-free" or "free-range." So what's the difference? And why should you care? As the name implies, "cage-free" means that animals are not confined to cages. While this is certainly better for their lives and our bodies than confinement, this is not actually a very meaningful term.

Cage-free animals still live their lives in tight quarters, away from sunlight, fresh air, and their natural diets. Similar to cage-free poultry, their "free-range" counterparts live most of their lives indoors. The key difference is that free-range animals have access to the outdoors, while cage-free animals do not.

The problem with this term is that you have no way to know how much time the animals actually spend outdoors, and whether the outdoor space is on grassy pasture, dirt, or even concrete!

From a nutrition and animal welfare point of view, pasture-raised poultry and eggs are the best choice. But just as we said earlier, the key is befriending farmers, so you can know firsthand how the animals are raised and what they are fed.

WILD-CAUGHT VS. FARM-RAISED SEAFOOD

When buying fish and seafood, the most important word to look for is "wild caught." This term means that the sea creature you are buying grew up in its natural habitat, eating the foods it evolved to consume. "Farm raised" seafood, on the other hand, is produced in small enclosures and fed unnatural diets, including food dyes to augment the fish's flesh, all of which can increase disease, leading many producers to use antibiotics (something you don't want in your seafood or your gut).

Regardless of which type of wild-caught seafood you choose, try to eat smaller fish that are lower on the food chain like sardines, salmon, tilapia, and shellfish like oysters and clams. This is because, sadly, many of the toxins now in our oceans build up in larger, predatory fish like tuna, shark, swordfish, and marlin.

WHEN TO PRIORITIZE ORGANIC AND WHY LOCAL FOODS?

ORGANIC VS. CONVENTIONAL

One of the most common words you will see at the store is "organic." But exactly what does this mean? Different countries have different regulations around the term, but in the United States, the "certified organic" label is only given to farmers who undergo annual audits to ensure they meet the following federal standards:

- No synthetic fertilizers or pesticides.

- No antibiotics, hormones or GMOs

- A host of other regulations about healthy land management and farming practices.

It's important to understand that "organic" produce is usually raised with fertilizers and pesticides, too. The difference is that conventional produce relies on synthetic chemicals, while organic produce makes use of less processed versions created from natural sources such as plant and animal waste. Regardless of whether you buy organic or conventional produce, I recommend washing your produce before eating it. More than 90% of conventional citrus fruits contain fungicides linked to hormone disruptions and cancers. Buying organic greatly reduces these disease contributors.

My best buying strategy is to make use of the Environmental Working Group's annual published "dirty dozen" and "clean fifteen" lists, found easily online. The dirty dozen lists the fresh foods contaminated with the most pesticides, based on the current USDA data and independent testing. Opposite the dirty dozen is the clean fifteen, the 15 fruits and veggies with the lowest amount of pesticide residues. When shopping for your household, I recommend buying as much produce on the dirty dozen, certified USDA organic. Save money on the clean fifteen items, buying conventional, if you cannot afford to spend on all organic fruits and vegetables, or if those are not available as certified USDA organic.

DIRTY DOZEN

As you can, prioritize purchasing organic.
1. Strawberries
2. Spinach
3. Kale, collard and mustard greens
4. Nectarines
5. Apples
6. Grapes
7. Cherries
8. Peaches
9. Pears
10. Bell and hot peppers
11. Celery
12. Tomatoes

CLEAN FIFTEEN

These items are generally safe for conventional purchase
1. Avocados
2. Sweet corn
3. Pineapple
4. Onions
5. Papaya
6. Sweet peas (frozen)
7. Eggplants
8. Asparagus
9. Broccoli
10. Cabbage
11. Kiwi
12. Cauliflower
13. Mushrooms
14. Honeydew melon
15. Cantaloupes

TIP: The "dirty dozen" and "clean fifteen" lists reflect testing of current fruits and veggies, so be sure to do a quick search for the most current list!

FIBER — WHAT IS IT? WHY DO WE NEED IT?

Fiber's the MVP you never knew you needed. Honest! Fiber impacts the body's blood sugar regulation, helps move toxins and excess hormones through the digestive tract, feeds good bacteria and increases the release of a fullness hormone, CCK.

Probiotics have gotten a lot of the spotlight when it comes to gut health - those are great, but without fiber, these good bacteria cannot do their job. Fiber also increases butyrate production, a "famous fat" that protects against cancer, Alzheimers, Parkinson's, prevents obesity and impacts inflammation. As the gut bacteria break down fiber, they produce butyrate.

Since fiber is largely indigestible, it also slows the rate that glucose or blood sugar, absorbs into the blood stream. In this way, fiber helps keep the body from having extreme highs and lows on your blood sugar curve, creating steady energy, less hormonal cravings, limiting insulin release and building overall metabolic health.

INCREASING FIBER INTAKE

SOLUBLE FIBER BENEFITS:

- Attracts water and turns into gel in the digestive tract
- Slows digestion
- Causes glucose to be released slowly
- Regulates blood sugar
- Reduces risk of heart disease
- Lowers total cholesterol
- Preferred fiber source if struggling with diarrhea

INSOLUBLE FIBER BENEFITS:

- Speeds food through the digestive tract
- Adds bulk to stools, preventing constipation
- Removes toxins and excess hormones more quickly from the body
- Reduces risk of colon cancer
- Helps to balance pH

FIBER SUPPLEMENTATION:

- Flaxseed
- Psyllium husk
- Acacia fiber

INSOLUBLE FIBER FOODS:

- Almonds
- Apples with skin
- Avocado
- Beans, lentils and legumes (kidney, black, garbanzo, edamame, split peas, lima, navy, white, etc.)
- Berries (blackberries, blueberries, raspberries, strawberries, etc.)
- Cocoa
- Coconut (grated flakes or flour)
- Dried apricots, prunes, raisins, dates and figs
- Flaxseeds
- Green peas
- Oat bran
- Okra
- Pears with skin
- Passionfruit
- Potatoes and sweet potatoes
- Radishes
- Rutabaga
- Spinach
- Sunflower seeds
- Turnips
- Walnuts
- Wheat bran and wheat germ
- Whole grains (barley, quinoa, sorghum, millet, amaranth, oatmeal and rye)

SOLUBLE FIBER FOODS:

- Apples
- Asparagus
- Avocado
- Beans including black, kidney, white, lima and navy beans, edamame, etc.
- Brussels sprouts, cabbage, broccoli and other cruciferous veggies
- Carrots
- Corn

- Dried figs, prunes, apricots and dates
- Flaxseeds
- Lentils and other legumes like green peas
- Macadamia nuts
- Oranges and nectarines
- Passion fruit
- Peaches
- Pears

- Psyllium husk
- Sweet potato
- Tofu and tempeh (fermented soy products)
- Turnips
- Whole grains like barley, oats/oat bran, amaranth, etc.

Still feel you're not getting enough fiber?
My favorite go-to fiber supplements are listed at www.heyheymaeclients.com by searching "fiber".

SOS DINNER GUIDE & RESTAURANT HACKS

Eating out is one of my most favorite pleasures in life. The people we dine with, the creatives who craft menus for a living, the bountiful food, rich atmospheres and more — dining out was a place I worked hard to navigate as my eating remodeled for the sake of my health. As with all things, I want to give you some specific suggestions and provide a framework to enable you to master dining out with ease.

Above all, remember that you are the client. You are paying the restaurant and more often than not - they are happy to serve you! Restaurants love to meet your needs, offer hospitality and safe dining for their customers. Speak up! Allergens and intolerances are more common and restaurants are more familiar with them. Servers can help you navigate menus to find foods that will fill you safely and enjoyably.

EATING OUT TIPS AND IDEAS:

- Steakhouses often have simple foods: order a protein with steamed veggies, a baked sweet or white potato without the fixins.

- You can always ask for your food to be prepared with no oil, thanks to many gallbladder surgeries in America, lots of folks already order foods this way. "No oil" helps me steer clear of soybean and seed oils when eating out.

- For fine dining, restaurants who boast farm-to-table or share a farm sourcing list are often committed to quality ingredients, transparency and will be more easily able to omit an ingredient from your meal's prep.

- Check online! Many chain restaurants have an allergen guide or App to quickly sort out your top allergens, leaving behind the foods you can choose from.

- Mexican restaurants are happy for your fajitas to be ordered with no oil, making your meal into meat, onions and peppers — pretty great and balanced with a bit of guacamole on the side for those healthy fats.

- Bring your own chips! I keep individual grain-free tortilla chips, plantain chips, sweet potato chips and potato chips cooked in avocado oil in my car. I'll tote these into my favorite Mexican restaurant, use them as crackers to scoop to-go chicken salad on or eat them with my lunch in place of the restaurant's standard chip, fried in trans fats.

- Mediterranean and Greek restaurants have lots of complex salads and fresh options with simple prepared proteins.

- BBQ restaurants with smoked meats are a great options. There will often be simply prepared green beans or greens as well as streamed veggies and almost always a salad you can top with your BBQ meat.

- Bring your own sauce. Ordering individual packets of clean dressings like Primal Kitchen and Tessamaes is easy online. I also keep small screw top, leak free containers in my kitchen to quick fill with a dressing, dip or drizzle from home when dining out.

- Individual coconut aminos and gluten free tamari are available to take with to your favorite sushi restaurant when avoiding gluten.

- Vietnamese is a great Asian dining option with less soy sauce and MSG — most pho bowls are gluten free, featuring rice noodles. This is my go-to cold, rainy weather or sick to-go food.

- Order your sandwich without bread, opting for a lettuce wrap instead. This makes lots of deli-style restaurants more accessible.

FAVE SNACK IDEAS:

- Smoothie with protein powder and healthy fats from a smoothie shop

- Cold-pressed juice

- To-Go guac with my car chips or a bag of baby carrots

- A hard boiled egg or fruit cup is an easy grocery or quick stop option

- Dill pickles can be found at many convenience stores and even Jimmy John's has a great, giant pickle

- Grab spring rolls from your fave Thai place

MEETING FOR COFFEE?

- Tea is an awesome option, there's typically honey available for that sweet touch.

- Order your tea iced and unsweetened. You can also add honey here if needed, which will greatly reduce the amount of sugar you'll drink in, while adding nutrition, too.

- Decaf coffee and plain black coffee is a great place to start. In some seasons, I'll pack a quality marshmallow or two or a little mix of my own dried coconut cream and coconut sugar for a quick DIY creamer of sorts.

- Cinnamon and cocoa are often available in shakers on the condiment bar and can add a special taste to standard coffee or tea.

- Be sure to ask if the oat, coconut, almond, or other non-dairy milk is gluten free. Further, barista blend non-dairy milks often use trans or hydrogenated fats as emulsifiers, making these milks best to avoid.

- Steamed milk can be a great option for a winter warm-up, particularly if your shops offers quality milks.

- Adding steamed milk to any tea creates a lovely little latte. Adding steamed milk to earl gray tea makes the popular London Fog drink.

- Bring your own bag! In seasons where my therapeutic diet made it best for me to bring my own options, I'd often buy my friend's drink and ask for an additional large cup of hot water. I'd drop my own tea bags in and enjoy, guilt free.

BOTTOM LINE OF EATING OUT?

You and only you can build your health. To ask for what you need, even if it's not typical or even a bit uncomfortable, is the best way to love and care for yourself. Your body is where you'll live when you're 90 — choice by choice we create long-term health.

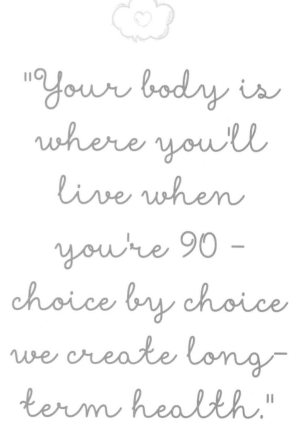

"Your body is where you'll live when you're 90 — choice by choice we create long-term health."

HOW TO SHOP & SAVE
AT THE GROCERY

Eating a diet full of nutrient-dense, whole foods can seem overwhelming and expensive. But, it can 100% work for you and your lifestyle. Grocery shopping and food prep does not have to take up your whole Sunday and half of your paycheck.

Remember, the kitchen is a special space in the home filled with laughter, community, and teachable moments. The kitchen is an honorable place — you get to steer the ship on your family's health — what power! It's the heart of the home, so let's keep it that way by kicking some of the stress of shopping and cooking to the curb. You can set yourself up for success and enjoy your adventure with food.

When implementing a new way of eating there will be some trial and error to find what works for you! Keeping a curious attitude will take you far!

TOP TIPS TO STAY WITHIN YOUR BUDGET:

- Meal plan! Write down each meal for the week including breakfast, lunch, and dinner. You can add some snacks in there, too, if that's helpful for you.

- Make a grocery list of all the ingredients you need. Go through your fridge/freezer/pantry FIRST that way you don't overspend on items you already have.

- For some it's helpful to avoid going to the store when hungry. This can lead to purchasing unnecessary items out of hanger.

- Prioritize organic purchases. Stick to organic for the Dirty Dozen and nonorganic for the Clean Fifteen.

- Buy in-season produce.

- Start your own vegetable or herb garden! Take it from me, it's so satisfying getting your hands in the dirt and harvesting your own food for meals. Gardening has been the second biggest tool, behind repeated exposures to an array of foods, when it comes to raising boys who love vegetables, fruits and herbs.

When the boys have helped to grow the foods, they're very eager to try them, create with them and help with cooking.

- Find a few go-to recipes and rotate through them. Swap out veggies and spices to mix it up.

- Buy pantry items in bulk.

- Meal prep. Meal prep doesn't have to be all or nothing. Figure out what will make your week go smoother (i.e. smoothie bags, clean and chop fruits and veggies before putting them in the fridge, batch cooking protein, etc.).

STAYING ORGANIZED WHEN SHOPPING IS ALSO SUPER HELPFUL, HERE'S HOW:

Buy bulk items from Costco or Sam's Club. Shop Aldi weekly, if saving on produce is important: several organic options available.

Buy produce from your local store or farmer's market. No need to buy produce in bulk if you don't plan to cook it all that week. I think we start out with good intentions to eat all the fruits and veggies so we LOAD UP....buuut then half of it goes in the trash. Buy what you need for produce to ensure you only take what you eat. If some remains and it can be frozen to add to smoothies, chop it up and toss in a freezer bag for later. I love to use zucchini, cucumbers, salad greens, cabbage and more in this way.

If possible, source your meat from a local farmer. More often than not the prices are better than the store, and you know how the animal was fed and raised. You can buy in bulk, buy products individually like at the grocery store or commit to a money-saving monthly meat CSA, too. The animal is also often raised on more quality, nutrient rich soils, which translate to nutrient value when you eat. Win-win.

Thrive Market is a great online shop for clean items if you can't find what you want locally.

GROCERY STORE TIPS:

- Rotisserie chicken to pull apart and use for multiple meals
- Premade salads
  - Swap the croutons and cheese for pumpkin seeds and cracked pepper
  - Swap the packaged dressing for olive oil & vinegar
- Frozen veggies instead of fresh
- Precut fruit
- Individual quinoa packets (Costco has these)
- Individual wild rice packets (Target has these)
- Individual oatmeal packets (Trader Joes has these)
- Purchase pantry items in bulk (coconut water, dried fruit, oils, beef jerky, nuts)
- Meal plan for the whole week or the first 3 days of the week

When the boys have helped to grow the foods, they're very eager to try them, create with them and help with cooking.

EASY DINNER IDEAS:

- Sheet pan meals

  - Add a protein
  - Green vegetable
  - Root vegetable

- Sheet Pan Combinations

  - Sweet Green Sheet Pan Dinner
  - Harvest Sheet Pan Dinner
  - Sausage, potatoes, brussel sprouts
  - Chicken breasts, asparagus, potatoes
  - Squash, sausage, broccoli
  - Broccoli, cauliflower, sweet potatoes, chicken
  - Chicken, tomatoes, green beans, potatoes

- Prep protein items in bulk over the weekend

- Batch cook soups or other crock pot meals (freeze and thaw when needed)

SIMPLE SNACKS:
(combine items to create a protein/carb/fat combo)

- Beef jerky

- Hard boiled eggs

- Pre-cut fruit

- Nut butter packets

- Sugar free applesauce or stewed apples

- Dried fruit

- Nuts

- Grass-fed cheese if tolerated

- Bone broth

- Pre make smoothies, frozen in ice cube trays

- Cut up apples to store in the fridge (coating apples with a small amount of lemon juice prevents oxidation)

EASY LUNCH IDEA:

- Turkey roll ups
- Salad w/ protein (salmon, chicken, pulled beef, instapot carnitas), olive oil and ACV dressing
- See snack ideas too, to add into lunches
- Veggies w/ hummus or guac
- Chicken/tuna/sardine salad on greens made with homemade or avocado oil mayo
- Charcuterie board style lunch, meat, veggies (radishes, carrots, zucchini, broccoli, cauliflower) guac, hummus, goat cheese, berries, etc

HYDRATE!

- Reusable water bottle
- Electrolyte packets
- Coconut water
- Bone broth
- Trace mineral drops
- Fruits and herbs for infusing (lemon, mint, cucumber, raspberries)

"You can set yourself up for success and enjoy your adventure with food."

GLUTEN-FREE, MOSTLY DAIRY-FREE MASTER SNACK LIST

The place I'm most likely to fall off the plan is at snack time. I tend toward repeating the same snacks, the same flavor profiles and thus the same nutrient profiles.

This snack list is wonderful to use for someone on a special diet — make a big list of what you CAN have to stay focused on all the options available. A great little guide for lunch-box packing and just a fun way to think differently about food, too. This is my most-used client resource.

At the end, you'll see a master list of all fruits and vegetables handy to us in the states. Doing the same with this list in healing seasons, writing up what you CAN have and removing what you are omitting for the time, helps our brains create dinners easily and stay away from dwelling on what's missing.

In my opinion, snacking has become somewhat demonized by the health industry and most in the diet industry write it off completely. Think about it, do you ever feel guilty for snacking? Where did that come from? It could be because most traditional snacks in the Standard American Diet are highly processed foods full of sugar, food dyes, and chemical additives.

Snacking can be mindless and full of empty calories OR nutritious, balanced, and used to balance blood sugar regulation.

If you picture your blood sugar cycles throughout the day like a fire it would look something like this: when we eat, we fuel that fire. If we go too long without, the fire will dwindle down and possibly go completely out. Eating an imbalance of macronutrients can also cause the fire to dwindle, explode or extinguish.

Eating higher-sugar snacks creates a fire that rages for a short time, burns up energy, creating a dysregulated mood and leaves you feeling feeble.

Protein and fat are the logs of the fire, meaning they provide longer lasting fuel and energy. Carbohydrates are the kindling that give us that quick burst of flames. We want to eat a combination of all three macronutrients to have a steady, slow-burning fire throughout the day. This will prevent sharp spikes and drops in blood sugar that leave us either too hyper or hangry and reaching for the nearest form of sugar.

Don't forget that when blood sugar is too high or too low, the body perceives it as stress. When under stress, the adrenal glands pump out cortisol and adrenaline. If blood sugar is too high, the muscle tissues and liver are signaled to store blood sugar.

Any remaining blood sugar is stored in fat tissue. When blood sugar is too low, the liver and muscle tissues are signaled to release stored glycogen to be recirculated as blood sugar. If the glycogen stores run out, the liver begins to break down tissue (amino acids) to be converted into new glucose through a process called gluconeogenesis.

So, how can we snack to ensure that we are properly fueling the fire of our blood sugar? The answer is food combining. A source of protein, carbohydrate, and fat should all be present in a snack, or at least 2 of these macronutrients. Bonus points for working greens and fiber in, especially at mealtime.

- Carbohydrate = quickest to digest, easy energy

- Protein = slower to digest, provides bulk to a snack (most of us struggle to eat enough protein throughout the day, so a few snacks containing protein can help with that!)

- Fat = slowest to digest, helps us feel full for longer, slows the digestion of carbohydrates when paired together

Snacks can be sugar bombs, but they most certainly don't have to be- combine those macronutrients.

Here's how I snack without sugar:
- Check out my Ultimate Gluten Free, Dairy Free Snack List (6 pages of snack ideas!).

- When in doubt stick to whole foods.

- Convenient foods like guacamole from a Mexican restaurant with carrots, or a hummus and veggie plate from a Mediterranean restaurant.

- Create a snack basket for your pantry with easy grab and go items. Stock it with snacks like jerky, nut butter packets, dried fruit, individual packets of nuts, and protein bars or collagen bars.

NUTS AND SEEDS

Acorn	Hazelnut
Almond	Hemp Hearts
Brazil	Macadamia
Cacao	Peanut
Cashew	Pecan
Cedar	Pine nuts
Chestnut	Pistachio
Chia	Pumpkin Seeds
Coconut	Sunflower Seeds
Flaxseeds	Walnut

NUT BUTTERS

Almond	Pecan
Cashew	Pumpkin
Coconut	Sunflower
Hazelnut	Walnut
Peanut	Watermelon

DIPS

Almond cheese spread	Hot Sauce
BBQ Sauce	Hummus
Buffalo sauce	Ketchup
Coconut Aminos	Mayonnaise
Dairy-free Pesto	Mustard (+ honey)
Dessert Hummus	Olive Tapenade
Everything bagel seasoning	Salad dressing
Garlic Ailoli	Salsa
Honey Mustard	Tahini

CARBY SNACKS

Frozen banana + oat pancake, toasted
GFDF Pretzels + dessert hummus
GFDF pretzels + dip
GFDF Pretzels + mustard
GFDF toast + avocado + drippy egg
Oatmeal
Popcorn
Protein oat balls
Sweet rice rollers + nut butter

Fresh SNACKS

Beet + goat cheese

Black olives + goat cheese inside

Bowl of Salad or Slaw

"Caprese" tomato slice + basil leaf + balsamic glaze

Carrots + hummus + sprinkle everything seasoning

Carrots + mustard + dash of honey

Celery + sunflower seed butter + dried cranberries

Cilantro guacamole dip: guac + bunch of cilantro leaves + clove garlic + avocado oil

Coconut Cream + fruit

Cultured coconut yogurt + fruit

Cole slaw

Guacamole

Jicama sticks or slices + dip

Kimchi

Marinated Artichokes

Marinated Asparagus

Pickles

Pickle roll up: pickle + deli meat + toothpick

Pico de Gallo

Radish + Butter + Salt

Raw broccoli + nut cheese dip

Sauerkraut

Spring rolls: julienned veggies, herbs, chicken or shrimp, wrapped in rice paper

Steamed + salted edamame + truffle oil drizzle

Sugar snap peas

Savory SNACKS

Bacon wrapped water chestnuts

Bone Broth

Celery + peanut butter + raisins

Cucumbers + goat cheese + dill

Cucumbers + tuna or egg salad

Deviled egg

Deli meat + pickle roll up

Fingerling potato slices + coco oil + salt; roasted

Giardiniera

GFDF toast + avocado + everything seasoning

Grain-Free Chip

Grass-fed Hot Dog

Hard boiled egg

Hummus + veggies

Kale chips

Marinated artichoke hearts

Meat jerky

Meat sticks

Meat stock

Peanuts in shell

Pickled cauliflower

Pickle spears

Pistachios

Plantain chips

Popcorn

Pork rinds

Radish + lime + salt

Rice cake + dip or nut butter

Roasted chickpeas

Salami + pickle roll up

Salami + pretzel roll up

Sardines + celery

Sardines + lemon squeeze

Seaweed

Sunflower seeds in shell

Sweet potato "toast" + avocado +everything seasoning

Tortilla chips

Tostones + guacamole

Veggies + bean dip

Whole dill pickle + on a stick

SWEET SNACKS

Apple nachos: apple sliced through core, nut butter, coconut, chia seeds, DF chocolate mini-chips

Applesauce

Apples + nut butter

Banana nachos: banana slices, nut butter, coconut, chia

Banana "nice cream" + almond butter + cocoa

Bacon wrapped date

Blueberries + watermelon + mint

Cinnamon Apples

Coconut whipped cream with fresh berries

Coconut cream over frozen berries + chia

Coconut milk + frozen berries popsicles

Coconut oil + cocoa powder or chocolate

Chia pudding: chia + almond milk + add ins: cocoa powder + cayenne OR lemon juice, zest + blueberries + toasted coconut

Corn tortilla, coconut or almond wrap, nut butter, rolled

Dates + goat cheese inside

Dates + nut butter inside + frozen

Date + butter + salt

Dehydrated apple chips

Dried banana chips

Dried Mango

Dried Apricots

Dried apricots + goat or sheep cheese

Fig wrapped in prosciutto

Frozen applesauce with a popsicle stick

Frozen blueberries

Frozen cherries

Frozen grapes

Frozen peach slices

Frozen fruit, coconut milk poured on top

Fruit kabobs

Fruit leather

Gelatin gummies (coconut whip + bee pollen)

GF granola

Grapes dipped in melted coconut butter

Green smoothie

Homemade gelatin gummies

Kettle corn

Mandarin Orange

Peach wrapped in prosciutto

Pineapple + deli ham skewers

Popsicles made from blended fruit and coconut water or milk

Protein smoothie

Watermelon + lime popsicles

Watermelon + mint (+ honey)

Yogurt Drops, frozen on parchment or wax paper

Yogurt (goat/nut based) + honey + chia + frozen fruit

Yogurt + protein powder bowl w/ mixed nuts or granola

Watermelon + mint

Watermelon + sheep's milk feta cheese

Veggies

Amaranth Leaves
Arrowroot
Artichoke
Arugula
Asparagus
Bamboo Shoots
Beans, Green
Beets
Belgian Endive
Bitter Melon
Bok Choy
Broadbeans
Broccoli
Broccoli Rabe
Brussel Sprouts
Cabbage, Green
Cabbage, Red
Carrot
Cassava
Cauliflower
Celeriac
Celery
Chayote
Chicory
Collards
Corn
Crookneck
Cucumber
Daikon

Dandelion Greens
Edamame, Soybeans
Eggplant
Fennel
Fiddleheads
Ginger Root
Horseradish
Jicama
Kale
Kohlrabi
Leeks
Lettuce, Iceberg
Lettuce, Leaf
Lettuce, Romaine
Mushrooms
Mustard Greens
Okra
Onion, Red
Onion
Parsnip
Peas, Green
Pepper, Green
Pepper, Sweet Red
Potato, Red
Potato, White
Potato, Yellow
Pumpkin
Radicchio
Radishes

Rutabaga
Salsify
Shallots
Snow Peas
Sorrel
Spaghetti Squash
Spinach
Squash, Butternut
Sugar Snap Peas
Sweet Potato
Swiss Chard
Tomatillo
Tomato
Turnip
Watercress
Yam Room
Zucchini

Fruits

Apple
Apricots
Avocado
Banana
Blackberries
Blackcurrant
Blueberries
Breadfruit
Cantaloupe
Cherimoya
Cherries
Clementine
Coconut
Cranberries
Feioja
Fig
Gooseberries
Grapefruit
Grapes

Guava
Honeydew Melon
Jackfruit
Jujube
Kiwi
Kumquat
Lemon
Lime
Longan
Loquat
Lychee
Mandarin
Mango
Mangosteen
Mulberries
Nectarine
Olive
Orange
Papaya
Passionfruit
Peaches
Pear
Persimmon
Pineapple
Pitanga
Plantain
Plums

Pomegranate
Prickly Pear
Prunes
Pummelo
Quince
Raspberries
Rhubarb
Sapodilla
Sapote
Soursop
Starfruit
Strawberries
Tamarind
Tangerine
Watermelon

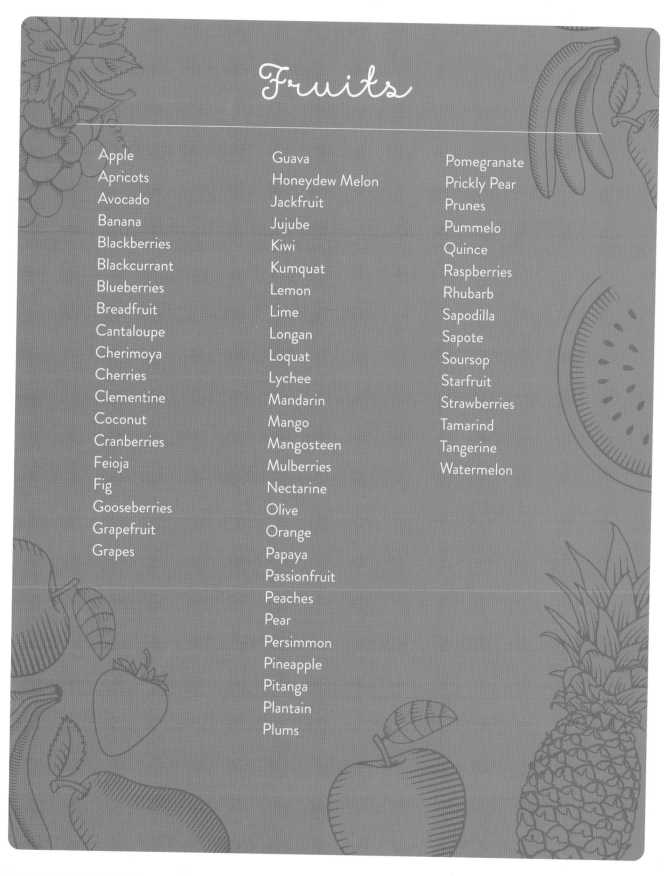

PART 2

hey hey

RECIPES

SIMPLE FOOD RULES

For food and feeding, I love simple rules that allow us to untangle all the food and diet messaging we've been bombarded with. Nutrition is this fascinating world because it's ever changing and research is spun out, continually. It's also so much in flux that discerning what to follow and which way to believe can be so hard. As much as new special diets and research can certainly inform better outcomes for individual bodies in specific situations, there are tried and true pillars of food and feeding. We'll focus on these pieces as we build our plates.

Special diets, studies and new biohacks: let's simplify. The biggest messages I want to engrave on our brains are these simple food rules:

1. Crowd in a variety of whole foods in their simplest forms onto your plate.

2. Good, better, best with food quality based on availability and budget.

3. Build every plate as an "Ideal Plate" that includes protein, fat, fiber, greens and a fermented food, if your body allows ferments; A snack to include 2 members of the "Ideal Plate."

4. Each day, aim for 7-9 cups fruits and veggies a day, 2 vegetables to 1 fruit ratio.

5. Do your best. Forget the stress. Next best choice, once choice at a time.

When I make dinner for my little fam, I try to consider these foundations above all else on a day-to-day basis. Foods aren't bad or off limits, we eat all things in balance. We explore foods as a fun adventure, whether at an international grocer, having the boys choose one fresh food we'll all try - no matter what - or exploring new recipes in other cuisines. Food is nourishment. Food is also joy and it's possible to create a simple framework to combine nourishment with joy! Feeding is the work we will do most in our life: think about it, we each eat 3+ times a day.

Choosing to uplevel our feeding skills so we are able to enjoy food and cooking will be so helpful and pay dividends in so many areas.

THE IDEAL PLATE

What to put on your plate at every meal; my favorite approach:

Macronutrient balance is the key to steady energy, improved digestion, as well as hunger and satiety, hormone balance. This ideal plate balance will keep you full, nourish your body and make maintaining a consistent weight, simple.

1. **Protein:** Proteins from animal meats and plant proteins like chickpeas, lentils and hemp option are more slowly digested by the body, allowing a steady release of blood glucose. This steady release makes for steady energy and less physical stress on the body. Protein also causes the release of Glucagon-Like-Peptide-1 (GLP-1) which signals fullness in the brain and the appetite controlling Peptide YY. Adequate protein keeps us fuller, longer while inadequate protein stimulates the release of neuropeptide Y (NPY) which promotes cravings for carbohydrates. Eat more protein, crave less carby foods? Seems easy enough!

2. **Fat:** Fats from animal proteins, animal fats, dairy products and plants like avocado, coconut and olives are slow digesters, too, releasing a steady stream of blood glucose. Fat also causes release of the two satiety hormones Leptin and Cholecystokinin (CCK). Fat also lowers fasting insulin levels and can double the production of CCK, telling your brain you're full, more quickly. CCK stimulates healthy digestion by provoking the gallbladder to contract and release stored bile into the intestines and secretion of digestive-aiding pancreatic juices. Fats create fullness and cleanse the digestive track!

3. **Fiber:** Fibers are found in many foods in both the soluble and insoluble form. Fiber physically stretches the stomach lining as it is consumed, turning off the hunger hormone Ghrelin, or "growlin'" as I often say. Fiber also feeds and nourishes the beneficial gut bacteria in the gastrointestinal track, allowing "good" bacteria to retain microbial balance, and bacterial production of energizing b-vitamins to continue. Fiber also slows down blood glucose release. This makes fiber a preventative factor for blood sugar disregulation as extreme as diabetes. Fiber also helps to end those hangry feels we can fall victim to.

4. **Greens:** Everything from the traditional kale, collards and spinach to brussels, broccoli and cabbage are considered greens - any non-starchy vegetable that stimulates your chewing and adds bulk to your meal, counts. Green veggies also increase GLP-1 levels, signaling fullness. The mineral-rich nutrients that greens provide nourish the microbiome and whole body.

   Bonus: Fermented food and/or a cup of bone broth

FOOD FOUNDATIONS

Keep in mind to build your meals with a variety of the following pilar foods included:

1. Quality filtered water
2. Mineral rich salt
3. Bone broth
4. Fermented foods like saurkrauts and kefir
5. Variety of Grass-fed and organic proteins
6. Rotate healthy fats: pastured lard, tallow, duck fat; olive, coconut, avocado oils etc.
7. Nutrient dense vegetables and fruits: dark leafy greens and deeply colored fruits and veggies (think a cherry or beet instead of an apple or cucumber)
8. Cooked and raw veggies, mostly cooked veggies in seasons of digestive distress
9. Grains and legumes, soaked and sprouted, when possible

We'll expand on these throughout the book, but focusing on these as strong foundations will greatly improve your health. I like to make light work of foods and feedings with pocket-sized information and these checklists are tops for easily learning a memorable way to nourish our families.

FOODS FOR OPTIMAL DIGESTION

1. **Colorful foods:** Foods like ginger, blueberries, blackberries, green tea and curry powder. These foods will reduce inflammation in the gut and also contain polyphenols. Polyphenols have beneficial effects throughout the body and specifically on the digestive system. Recent research around polyphenols show they help regulate energy metabolism and overall digestive health.
2. **Green Leafy Veggies:** Leafy veggies include spinach, kale and swiss chard. These foods are high in naturally occurring folate, which helps offset antidepressant medications and can help prevent digestive tract cancers. Leafy greens also provide fiber and magnesium to your diet. Greens also feed your good gut bacteria. You want to aim for at least 25% leafy greens and 25% cooked veggies at every meal.
3. **Fiber:** Apples, gluten-free oats and lentils, psyllium husk, peas and seeds (hemp, flax, chia, pumpkin) are fiber rich foods. Fiber helps regulate your bowel movements and feed your gut bacteria. Most carbs, proteins and fats are absorbed into the bloodstream before they make it to the large intestine, leaving little for the gut flora. Insoluble fiber feeds those gut flora in the large intestine.
4. **Bone broth:** Make your own or look for brands like Epic, Kettle and Fire and Bonafide. Bone broth is a digestive aid that helps support and promote healing in the gut. Pages 248-249 will provide you with recipes for how to make your own. You can also now purchase quality bone broth in nearly all grocery stores. Bone broth also reduces inflammation and contains amino acids like glycine and glutamine that help keep your gut working properly, which aids in digestion and keeps your immune system in check.
5. **Crowd it out:** Focus on crowding out your foods. Not on eliminating completely. This concept is about adding in more of the good stuff first.

A Word About DIGESTION

"All disease begins in the gut…" - Hippocrates

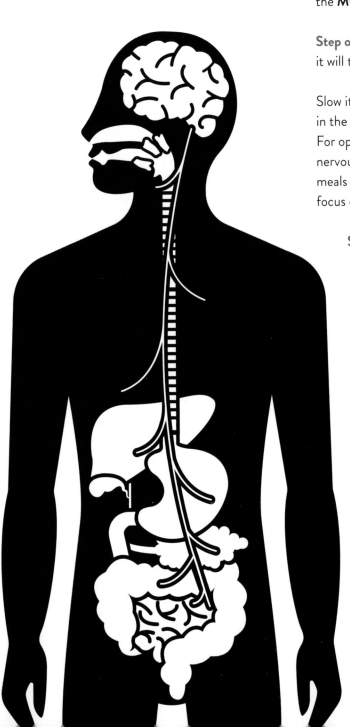

One more thing before we start cooking! Without proper, even optimal digestion, we can not create nor maintain health. How does digestion work?

Digestion begins in the **BRAIN** and digestive action starts in the **MOUTH**.

Step one: look at your food, give thanks for it, think about how it will taste. Smell your food. Ready?

Slow it down, sister. The body doesn't digest our foods when in the sympathetic nervous system state or "fight or flight". For optimal digestion, the body must be in the parasympatheic nervous system state or "rest and digest". When we eat our meals at a slow rate, in a relaxed and rested state, our body will focus on optimally digesting every bite.

Step two: Take 5-6 deep breaths, until you feel your shoulders relax and your mouth salivate.

Mechanical digestion begins in the mouth…where there are teeth. **THERE ARE NO TEETH IN YOUR STOMACH!**

Step three: Chew your food to an applesauce consistency, 20-30 chews per bite.
When we don't chew, our brain doesn't get the message to begin chemical digestion in other parts of the digestion process. When we don't properly digest our food, nutrient absorption doesn't occur. Chewing signals digestive secretions!

Step four: Have a small cup of water with your meal, allowing digestive secretions to concentrate on your food. Mindful eating: check. Rest and digest: check. Chewing: check. Concentrated secretions: check. All done?

SLOW IT DOWN, SISTER!

Eat that meal slowly and you will be optimized at every turn. Plenty of time to chew, more time to breathe, a continued state of relaxation, concentrated digestive secretions on every bite of food: digestive success starts here.

Step five: Enjoy your meal over 30 minutes.
Modeling this for our children is my number one health builder. Choosing to do this, ourselves, is the biggest digestive healer. What happens when we don't eat with digestion in mind?

WHAT DOES PARTIALLY DIGESTED FOOD DO IN MY GI TRACT?
CARBOHYDRATES —-> FERMENT
PROTEINS —--> PUTRIFY
FATS —----> RANCIDIFY

ALL UNDIGESTED FOOD ROTS IN THE GI TRACT
Chew your food. Think about my favorite teaching lesson: I toss a bunch of food into a blender, spin her up until it all looks like applesauce. Pop the top on and sit that blender on the sidewalk at 98.9°F or into your oven at 100°F. Leave it for 4-5 hours, the average time it takes for food to reach the intestines. What happens? Food starts bubbling, smelling not so great. Leave the partially digested food for 24-72 hours, the average time from bite to stool and see what happens. I'll give you a hint: it's nasty.

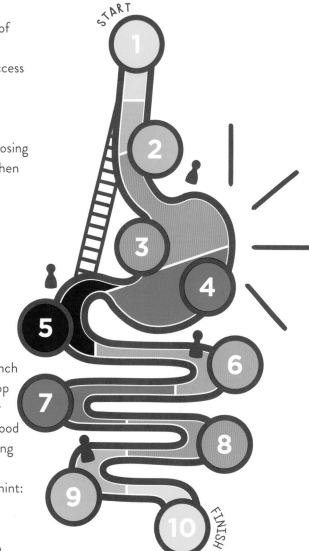

Digestive secretions are what allow food to turn from applesauce into nourishing energy. Any undigested food will continue to wreak havoc on your digestive tract, where the temp is a constant 98.9°F or so.

DIGESTIVE CHECKLIST
Simple steps to help your digestion get the best start possible:
1. Eat in a parasympathetic state. We only digest in a parasympathetic (rest and relax, NOT fight or flight) state. This is a simple thing that is often a HUGE key to healing. Sit down and relax, practice gratitude, take a few deep breaths before taking your first bite. Look at your food and think about eating - begin eating AFTER salivation begins. No phones, no working, nothing but eating your meal.
2. Put your fork down between bites: promote your rest and digest state.
3. Chew each bite 20-30 times, swallowing only once the bite of food has reached a water-like consistency.
4. Drink sips of water, saving the bulk of your hydration between meals. This prevents you from watering down your digestive juices.
5. Stay seated for your whole meal.
6. 25-30 minute mealtimes are your goal, sitting down.

hey hey
BREAKFAST

SWEET POTATO BREAKFAST CASSEROLE

Serves: 12 • Prep Time: 20 minutes • Cook Time: 40 minutes

● PALEO ● GRAIN-FREE ● **GUT HEALTH** ● **NUTRIENT DENSE**

This recipe may very well be my most favorite of the book! It's the new-mom dropoff gift to a friend, it warms our bellies on Christmas morning and wins MVP on my weekday breakfast reheat rotation. If you try one recipe, try this breakfast casserole.

ingredients

- 2 tablespoons coconut oil for greasing the dish
- 2 medium sweet potatoes sliced into ½ inch rounds
- ¼ cup healthy fat for cooking
- 6 slices bacon
- 1 medium onion, finely chopped
- 1 clove garlic
- sea salt to taste
- 10 ounces organic fresh baby spinach or power greens
- ½ cup sliced mushrooms of choice

- 8 ounce jar artichoke hearts, drained and chopped
- 12 large pasture raised eggs
- ½ cup full-fat canned coconut milk
- ½ teaspoon salt
- ¼ teaspoon black pepper
- ¼ teaspoon onion powder
- 2 tablespoons nutritional yeast

instructions:

1. Preheat oven to 400°F and grease a 9 by 13-inch casserole dish with coconut oil (or ghee).
2. Toss sweet potato rounds in fat of your choice to coat (I love lard, here), salt to taste and arrange on the bottom of casserole dish, overlapping slightly. Place in the oven to soften and bake for 20 minutes.
3. Place bacon in a cold cast iron skillet and turn on to medium-low. After crisping bacon, remove onto paper towels to cool.
4. Begin sautéing onions and garlic in bacon grease until onions are caramelized, salting as necessary. Caramelization of the onions might take 20 minutes, but is worth the wait!
5. Add the spinach and mushrooms to the onions and garlic, salting again and allowing the spinach to wilt, then add the artichoke hearts. Once warmed through, remove from heat.
6. In a large bowl, whisk together eggs, coconut milk, salt, pepper, onion powder, and nutritional yeast, until very smooth.

SWEET POTATO BREAKFAST CASSEROLE CONT.

instructions continued:

7. After the sweet potatoes are finished roasting in the oven, distribute onion, spinach, mushroom and artichoke mixture over the potato base.
8. Crumble the cooked bacon evenly on top of the spinach mixture, now in the casserole dish.
9. Lastly pour the egg mixture into the casserole dish, spreading evenly.
10. Return to the oven and cook for 30-35 minutes, until the egg mixture sets in the center and begins to puff up.
11. Serve while warm. You can store the leftovers in the refrigerator to reheat during the week for a quick breakfast!

NEW TO NUTRITIONAL YEAST?

Nutritional yeast is used as a cheese replacement!
This is not the same type of yeast that allows baked goods to rise. It is a complete protein, and contains B vitamins specifically folate, thiamine, riboflavin, niacin, selenium and zinc!
Nutritional yeast is considered anti-viral, anti-bacterial and boosts the immune system, while improving digestion!

MINI ZUCCHINI BASIL FRITTATAS

Serves: 2 • Prep Time: 15 minutes • Cook Time: 30 minutes
● **PALEO** ● GRAIN-FREE

ingredients

- 4 eggs
- 1 cup shredded zucchini or squash
- ¼ cup basil, cut into ribbons
- pinch of garlic powder
- pinch of turmeric (optional)
- dash salt, pepper
- coconut oil for oiling up ramekins

instructions:

1. Preheat your oven to 350°F. Lightly oil two small ramekins with coconut oil and set aside.
2. Crack two eggs in each ramekin and lightly beat with a fork. Add in cut up basil and zucchini, keep beating or whisking until mixed. Add in seasonings and lightly stir. You can also mix these in a separate bowl, if you prefer.
3. Place ramekins on a baking sheet and bake for 25-30 mins.
4. Serve warm or frittatas can be kept in the fridge for 3-4 days for easy reheating.

Pro Tip:

Double this recipe and you've got an easy breakfast for a few weekday mornings! To reheat, place on the counter while the oven heats up. Pop in for 4-5 minutes, until warmed through.

BREAKFAST MEATLOAVES

Serves 4 • Prep Time: 3 minutes • Cook Time: 10 minutes

● PALEO ● GRAIN-FREE ● **NUTRIENT DENSE**

ingredients

- 1 pound ground pork, turkey, beef or ancestral blend
- ½ cup sweet onion, diced very fine
- 1 - 2 cloves of garlic
- 1 tablespoon Italian seasoning
- ¼ teaspoon salt
- ⅛ teaspoon black pepper
- Optional: ¼ cup cooked rice or ⅛ cup breadcrumbs

instructions:

1. Preheat oven to 375°F.
2. Mix all ingredients together.
3. Form into 8 little loaves.
4. Cook on a parchment lined baking sheet until the thermometer reads 140°F.
5. Top with a bit of ketchup or can fire roasted san marzano tomatoes sent through the blender for the remainder of cooking until internal temp is 160°F.
6. Enjoy!

HAM AND EGG CUPS

Serves 6 • Prep Time: 10 minutes • Cook Time: 15 minutes

● **PALEO** ● GRAIN-FREE

ingredients

- 8-10 pieces ham (I prefer to use canadian bacon)
- ½ cup goat cheese (optional)
- 12 egg whites **or** 6 full eggs
- 1 tablespoon water
- Salt and pepper, dash garlic powder to taste if veggies are not seasoned
- 1 cup chopped veggies (I like roasted broccoli)

instructions:

1. Preheat oven to 400°F degrees. Place a water bath into the stove - a baking pan or casserole dish filled with water.
2. Place ham slices into a muffin tin.
3. Whip eggs or egg whites whites with water, seasonings, and veggies.
4. Pour egg mixture into ham cups & bake for 15 - 17 minutes (less time if you plan to store in the refrigerator).

Pro Tip:

These are a quick and easy reheat on weekday mornings, popped into a warm oven or air fryer.

CITRUS & THYME TURKEY BREAKFAST SAUSAGE

Serves: 4 • Prep Time: 10 minutes • Cook Time: 15 minutes

● **PALEO** ● GRAIN-FREE

ingredients

- 1 tablespoon coconut oil, lard **or** bacon fat
- 1 pound ground turkey
- 2 tablespoons fresh thyme (or less dried thyme) **or** rosemary
- 1 tablespoon lemon **or** orange juice
- Zest from 1 lemon **or** orange
- Pinch salt to taste

instructions:

1. Mix ground meat with the thyme, zest, and salt. Combine well and form into small round patties (think flat sliders). You should have approximately 8 or so and the flatter you make them, the faster they'll cook.

2. Heat oil over medium heat in a sauté pan and add your patties (you may need to do this in batches). Cook for 3-4 minutes on each side. Serve with your favorite veggies, salad, or however you'd like them! Store for a week in the refrigerator.

Pro Tip:

TIP: You can also make them in a meatball shape when storing for later. Get a good crust on the outside and you'll have a little space for more cooking at reheat.

TIP: Lemon and thyme marry well, as do orange and rosemary, though they can be switched up,easily.

TIP: I often serve this over greens with shredded carrot or pan fried red cabbage and onions. I love to sub the thyme for rosemary or herbs de provence, too!

BREAKFAST BURRITO

Makes 6 burritos • Prep Time: 10 minutes • Cook Time: 15 minutes

● **PALEO** ● GRAIN-FREE ● **NUTRIENT DENSE**

ingredients

- ½ pound ground sausage, any variety
- 6 eggs
- 1 ½ cups leftover veggies
- Flatbread (recipe next page)

instructions:

1. Brown ground sausage over medium heat.
2. Scramble eggs, adding greens or veggies if you choose.
3. Warm remaining leftover veggies.
4. Warm flatbread.
5. Assemble burrito style and serve with salsa, hey hey ranch, or hot sauce. Enjoy!

Helpful Tip:

I love to add roasted sweet potatoes to these to add some heft and top with a bit of guac to work in some easy fats.

Double or triple this recipe to have weekday burritos. Lightly cook your eggs, assemble and wrap in parchment, then tin foil. Toss in the freezer to store. The night before, move burrito to the fridge. When ready to eat, heat in a 350°F oven or air fryer until warm and perfect for breakfast on the go.

Helpful
Tip:

These are fantastic
vehicles for just about
anything. Some
mornings we add
cinnamon apples and
cooked bacon. Other
days, I grab one stored
in the fridge and make
a quick turkey lunch
wrap. You can also
stack them with a thin
layer of jam between
layers, making an
allergy friendly cake
of sorts.

FLATBREAD

Serves 4-6 flatbreads • Prep Time: 3 minutes • Cook Time: 10 minutes

● **PALEO** ● GRAIN-FREE

ingredients

- ¼ cup coconut flour
- ½ cup arrowroot flour
- 1 cup full fat coconut milk
- 1 tablespoon pastured lard, chilled
- 1 teaspoon salt

instructions:

1. Mix flours and salt together.
2. Cut in lard with a pastry cutter or fork until pea sized.
3. Mix in coconut milk. Batter will look like wallpaper paste.
4. Heat cast iron pan or skillet to medium heat.
5. Pour ⅓ cup of batter into pan. Once in the pan, batter will look like pancake batter. Smooth with spatula to spread.
6. Pour ⅓ cup of batter into pan, spreading out with the back of a spoon or a twirl of the pan.
7. Allow to cook 2 -3 minutes on each side. Lower heat if necessary to allow batter to cook through.
8. Enjoy warm!

BACON, EGG AND LOW-CARB WAFFLE FEAST

Serves: 2 • Prep Time: 8 minutes • Cook Time: 20 minutes

● **PALEO** ● GRAIN-FREE ● **NUTRIENT DENSE**

ingredients

- 1 tablespoon coconut oil, lard **or** bacon fat
- 2 eggs, divided yolks and whites
- 2 tablespoons coconut flour
- ½ teaspoon baking powder
- 2 tablespoons coconut milk
- 2 scoops collagen powder (optional)
- pinch salt
- 4 slices bacon (nitrate-& sugar-free)
- 2-4 eggs

instructions:

1. Heat waffle iron and have ingredients ready (when working with egg whites, time matters.)
2. Beat egg whites until stiff peaks form (by hand it takes longer but also feels like a mini-workout.)
3. Add coconut flour, baking powder, coconut milk, and whisk into the stiff egg whites. Batter will look like a paste.
4. Add the yolks and whisk well. Lastly, if using, add collagen, salt. Mix well and you now have a nice batter.
5. You'll have approximately ⅔ cup of batter, divide as necessary for your iron. This made one full waffle using ⅓ cup. I heated mine to 4 on a scale to 5 and they were perfect.
6. Keep warm while making bacon and eggs. Add them to the top or sandwich inside the layers.

EVERYDAY WAFFLES

Serves: 3 - 10-inch waffles • Prep Time: 10 minutes • Cook Time: 30 minutes

● **PALEO**

ingredients

- 1 ¾ cups gluten free flour
- 3 teaspoons (grain free) baking powder
- ½ teaspoon salt
- 2 beaten egg yolks
- 1 ¾ cups coconut **or** almond milk
- ½ cup melted coconut oil **or** palm shortening
- 2 stiffly beaten egg whites
- Coconut oil for greasing the waffle iron

instructions:

1. Heat waffle iron.
2. In one bowl, sift together dry ingredients.
3. In another bowl, combine yolks, milk and oil; stir into dry ingredients.
4. Stiffly beat egg whites until they form stiff peaks.
5. Fold in whites, leaving a few fluffs amidst the batter.
6. Lightly grease your waffle iron with coconut oil. Pour ½-⅓ cup waffle batter into iron and cook until lightly golden brown.

Pro Tip:

(For kids) Make some waffles with chocolate chips and toss in the freezer. These can easily be toasted for quick breakfasts.

(For Moms) Make some plain ones that can be toasted or sprinkle in Everything But the Bagel Seasoning and use as bread for breakfast sandwiches.

PANTRY PANCAKE MIX

Makes So Many! • *Prep Time: 10 minutes* • *Cook Time: 20 minutes*

● **PALEO**

We love to mix up the dry ingredients in bulk to have on hand for easy pancake mornings whenever we want. These cook up nice and high, making them a solid biscuit sub. I've been known to freeze them individually with some scrambled egg and sausage inside, wrapped in parchment paper and aluminum foil. Toss in the fridge the night before, quickly heat in the oven or air fryer.

ingredients

- 4 ½ cups of gluten free flour
  (My favorite is Bob's Red Mill 1:1 Baking Flour or Costco's Namaste Gluten Free Flour)
- ½ cup ground flax seed
- 2 tablespoons baking soda
- 2 tablespoons baking powder
- 1 tablespoon cinnamon (if you'd like)
- 3 scoops collagen peptides

Mix all dry ingredients together and store in a sealed container in your pantry. A great kindergarten assignment for learning measuring and fun. I prefer to sift to combine.

When you're ready for an easy pancake morning, whisk together:

1 cup of dry mix
2 eggs
½ cup of water or milk or almond milk

1. If the mixture is too dense, and doesn't easily drip off the spoon in a thick stream, add a bit more of your choice liquid until the batter is a thick pancake batter consistency.
2. You can add some chocolate chips, sprinkles, blueberries or vanilla, cinnamon to the cooking batter. The sky's the limit, really.
3. These fry up best in coconut oil, heated medium-high on a griddle or cast iron pan.

Helpful Tip:

Turn your oven to 350°F and lightly coconut oil a pie dish. Pour batter into pie dish and bake for ~ 30 minutes, until fluffy. Once done serve it up like a pizza! I love to drop blueberries on top and 1 tablespoon of coconut or cane sugar for a crispy top. This is my "lazy Saturday mom" dish I'll cook on Friday night so the boys can easily grab a slice the following morning at their leisure, while I read in my bed. Alone.

ULTIMATE
MOM
SURVIVAL
TOOL!

MOM'S MULTITASKING MUFFINS

Makes 12 muffins • Total Time: 45 minutes

This muffin is my go-to Mom-survival recipe. It's flexible, they come out great every time, they're full of nourishment and free of both gluten and dairy.

You'll want to use gluten free oats, because conventional oats are often sprayed at the end of growth to prepare them for a quick harvest. I love a sprouted oat like One Degree Organics and find the oats blend down very easily to oat flour in my Vitamix.

During the summertime I grate, strain and freeze cups of zucchini in large muffin cups, then store the zucchini pucks in a freezer bag.

ingredients

- 2 ½ cups oats
- 1 tablespoon psyllium husk
- 1 tablespoon ground cinnamon
- 1 teaspoon baking soda
- 1 ½ teaspoon apple cider vinegar
- ¼ teaspoon salt
- ¾ cup unsweetened applesauce **or** mashed banana or canned pumpkin
- ¼ cup coconut **or** almond milk
- ⅓ cup honey* **or** maple syrup or sorghum
- 3 large eggs
- ¼ cup coconut oil, melted **or** avocado oil
- ½ tablespoon pure vanilla extract
- ⅓ cup chocolate chips **or** blueberries **or** granola **or** cranberries **or** other mix-in
- 1 cup grated zucchini

under 1-year-old, skip the honey

instructions:

1. Turn oven to 350°F and line a muffin tin with 12 liners.
2. If fresh grating zucchini, grate, place in the center of a clean dishtowel, squeezing out as much moisture as possible. Set to the side.
3. Pour 2 cups of oats in the blender (or all, if you prefer a smooth texture muffin) and pulse until very finely ground and flourlike. Add any remaining oats you reserved.
4. Add all remaining ingredients except mix ins and zucchini. Blend until smooth, stopping to wipe the blender sides as needed.
5. If using frozen zucchini, add to blender and blend until broken up. If using fresh zucchini, fold in the batter.
6. Fold in your mix-in of choice. If using blueberries, I like to toss them with a bit of oat or gluten free flour before mixing in, to keep them from leaking all over the batter. Adding lemon zest to compliment blueberries or orange zest to compliment cranberries or even apple chunks with an extra tablespoon of cinnamon are all great choices. Banana with walnut and some chocolate chips on top are another favorite of my boy's.
7. Portion batter between the muffin cups, sprinkling a bit of extra topping on top, as desired. Sometimes, I'll mix a bit of coconut sugar with cinnamon and dust the tops with this mixture - you do you - these are forgiving and flexible.
8. Bake for 20-25 minutes (fruit adds 3-5 minutes to cook time) or until a toothpick inserted in the middle comes out clean.
9. Remove muffins from tin and cool for 15 minutess on a cooling rack. Once cooled, muffins can be stored in an airtight container, kept in the fridge for up to 3-4 days.

Helpful Tip:

REFRIGERATE!

These will spoil quickly if not kept in the fridge. They keep in the freezer for a month! I love to toss a frozen one in the boys' lunchbox to keep things cold and have a little snack at lunch or for the ride home from school.

STRAWBERRY DONUTS

Serves: 6 • Prep Time: 10 minutes • Cook Time: 10-12 minutes

ingredients

- ¼ cup coconut **or** almond milk
- 1 teaspoon apple cider vinegar
- ¼ teaspoon vanilla extract
- ¼ cup pure maple syrup or honey
- 3 ½ tablespoons coconut, olive **or** avocado oil
- 1 cup gluten free all-purpose flour (I like Bob's Red Mill and Costco's Gluten-Free)
- 1 teaspoon (grain free) baking powder
- ¼ teaspoon salt
- ½ cup finely chopped strawberries

instructions:

1. Preheat oven to 350°F. Grease donut pan with coconut oil.
2. In a bowl combine wet ingredients (first 5). Set aside.
3. In a separate bowl, stir together remaining ingredients except for strawberries.
4. Pour wet mix into dry mix and stir until just combined. Don't overmix.
5. Fold in strawberries.
6. Scoop batter into prepared donut pan. It will be thick, distribute evenly.
7. Bake for 10-12 minutes, until lightly golden. Let cool on the cooling rack for 5-10 minutes. Flip pan and enjoy donuts!

These can be made in a mini-muffin tin, too!

DUTCH BABY (2-WAYS)

Serves: 5-6 • Prep Time: 5 mins • Cook Time: 15 mins

● **PALEO**

SWEET APPLE BABY

ingredients

- 4 tablespoons coconut oil
- 2 apples, cored and thin-sliced - (I like granny smith and gala)
- 2 tablespoons coconut sugar
- ¼ teaspoon fine sea salt
- 2 teaspoon vanilla extract
- 2 tablespoons ground cinnamon
- 5 eggs
- ⅔ cup canned full-fat coconut milk
- ¾ cup gluten free flour

instructions:

1. Preheat oven to 425°F.
2. Melt coconut oil in a 8-10 inch cast iron pan, over medium heat. Add apple slices, 1 tablespoon coconut sugar, a pinch of salt, 1 teaspoon of vanilla and cinnamon. Cook 4-5 minutes, until apples begin to brown. Spread apples in an even layer on the bottom of the pan.
3. While apple mixture is cooking, blend remaining coconut sugar and vanilla, salt, eggs, coconut milk and gluten free flour until smooth.
4. Pour over apples in hot cast iron pan and place whole pan in oven.
5. Bake for 10-15 minutes without opening the oven, until the edges are browned but not burnt. Remove and serve immediately. This is impressive when pulled from the oven and naturally deflates over time. I like to place a plate on top of the pan and very carefully flip her over.

CLASSIC BABY

ingredients

- 1 cup gluten free flour
- 1 cup coconut milk
- ½ teaspoon salt or to taste
- 4-6 eggs, fewer for lighter result and more for more density
- ½ cup coconut oil or lard or bacon grease

instructions:

1. Place an 8-10 inch cast iron skillet in the oven and preheat to 425°F.
2. Combine flour, milk, salt, and eggs using an immersion blender to make a thin batter.
3. Once the oven is pre-heated, add coconut oil to the hot skillet. Return the skillet to the oven to let the oil heat up and coat the entire skillet.
4. Pour the batter into the skillet and bake for 15 minutes. Do not open the oven door while cooking: you will know it's done when the baby's all puffed up and golden brown.

💡 Helpful Tip:

- Serve with maple syrup or maple butter - we add coconut whipped cream for celebratory breakfasts. My boys love to cut this in pizza slices and store in the fridge for a "cold apple pizza" snack. Must be stored in the fridge to keep 2-3 days.
- She is DIVINE served with bacon.

hey hey
SMOOTHIES

HOW TO BUILD A SMOOTHIE

Smoothies have fit in my solo mom life like carryout on a Friday night. I love starting my day with a smoothie and mostly because of what the smoothie has to offer, nutritionally.

Smoothies are:

- filling and blood sugar balancing
- full of nutrition to energize your day
- quick to blend up

- easy for busy mornings
- can be prepared in advance

LIQUID

Limitless GREENS

1-2 T FIBER

1-2 T FAT

1 Serving PROTEIN

1/4 c. FRUIT

YOU'VE GOT OPTIONS!

LIQUID
Coconut milk or cream, almond milk, macadamia milk, cashew milk, hemp milk. water, ice, coconut water, beet juice, pomegranate juice, coffee or espresso

GREENS
Frozen or fresh: spinach, romaine, mixed or power greens salad mix, zucchini, cauliflower, cucumber, butternut squash, pumpkin puree

FIBER
Psyllium husk, flax seed, acacia fiber, chia seed, avocado

FAT
Almond butter, cashew butter, peanut butter, sunflower butter, pumpkin butter, tahini, MCT oil, coconut oil, coconut manna, avocado

PROTEIN
Bone broth protein powder, whey protein powder, pea protein powder, hemp protein powder, hemp hearts, collagen

FRUIT
Frozen or fresh blueberries, cherries, peaches, raspberries, strawberries, mango, pineapple, banana, dragonfruit

BASIC SHAKE RECIPE

ingredients

In a blender, combine:
- 1 cup water, unsweetened coconut milk, 3-4 cubes of ice, more for a thicker shake
- 1 tablespoon fat - nut butter, tahini, mct oil, flaxseed oil
- 1 serving of protein powder / collagen powder / bone broth protein
- 1 scoop of fiber supplement of your choice or 1-2T fiber (acacia, chia, psyllium, flax)
- ¼ cup low-glycemic fresh or frozen fruit (such as berries)
- 1-2 cups greens

SIMPLE SMOOTHIE FORMULAS

STRAWBERRY TWIST
ingredients

- ½ cup strawberries
- ½ cup freshly juiced carrots

BANANA BERRY BUMP
ingredients

- ¼ cup blueberries
- ¼ cup strawberries

PUMPKIN PIE SMOOTHIE
ingredients

- ½ banana
- ½ cup organic pumpkin
- Hefty pinch each of ginger and cinnamon
- Dash of ground cloves

BERRY CITRUS SPLASH
ingredients

- ½ cup blackberries, blueberries, **and/or** strawberries
- Juice from 1 freshly squeezed orange

COZY APPLE CINNAMON
ingredients

- 1 medium apple
- ½ banana
- 1 teaspoon cinnamon

See:

The options are limitless and you can make them just like my Grandma Glad did - "look ma, no recipe!" Until you are ready to "toss and go" with your smoothie routine, try some of my favorite smoothie recipes!

Pro Tip:

To keep your blender running smoothly, add ingredients in the following order: liquid, fresh veggies and fruits, protein powders, nut butters, fiber, frozen fruits and veggies, ice. If the blender struggles, simply add a bit of water until it runs smoothly.

CINNAMON ROLL SMOOTHIE

ingredients

- 1 cup almond milk
- 1 cup loose leaf spinach
- 1 serving vanilla protein powder
- 2 dried dates, pit removed
- 2 teaspoons cinnamon
- 1 tablespoon ground flax
- Pinch of salt

Helpful Tip:

WANT A THICKER SMOOTHIE?

Use frozen fruit, frozen coconut water or nut milk cubes and less liquid. Chia seeds also add thickness.

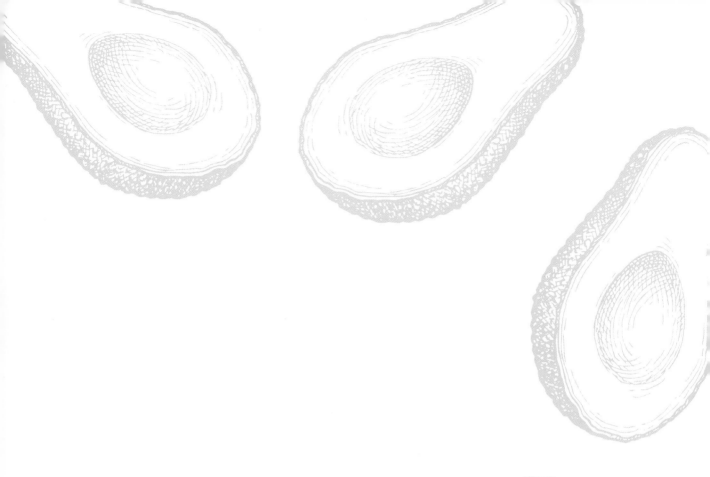

CHOCOCADO SMOOTHIE

ingredients

- 1 cup water
- 1 cup romaine (or spinach)
- ¼ cup frozen zucchini **or** cauliflower
- ½ avocado, fresh **or** frozen
- 1 serving chocolate protein powder
- 1 scoop chocolate **or** unflavored collagen
- 1 tablespoon cacao powder
- 1 tablespoon almond butter (**or** sunflower butter **or** peanut butter)
- 1 teaspoon cacao nibs (topping)

Helpful
Tip:

Use frozen fruit,
vegetables or
coconut milk to keep
your smoothie cold.

CHOCOLATE COVERED STRAWBERRY

ingredients

- 1 cup almond milk
- 1 cup spinach
- 1 tablespoon MCT oil
- 1 serving chocolate protein powder
- 1 tablespoon cocoa powder
- ½ cup ripe strawberries (you can leave the tops on)
- 1 tablespoon ground flax

ENERGIZING COFFEE SMOOTHIE

ingredients

- 1 cup brewed coffee (chilled or frozen into ice cubes)
- 1 cup spinach
- 1 serving chocolate protein powder
- 1 scoop chocolate collagen powder
- 1 tablespoon cocoa powder
- 2 tablespoons tahini or almond butter
- ⅓ avocado
- 2 tablespoons of seeds, such as flax, sunflower, **or** pumpkin
- Coconut milk **or** almond milk, even ice to your preferred thickness

Helpful Tip:

I love to add peppermint leaves or oil here for a peppermint mocha vibe, cacao nibs for texture or cinnamon powder and a pinch of ginger and cloves for a dirty chai vibe.

CHOCOLATE PEPPERMINT SMOOTHIE

ingredients

- ½ cup coconut **or** almond milk
- ½ cup water
- 1 cup frozen zucchini
- ¼ cup frozen cherries
- 1 tablespoon chia seeds
- 1 scoop collagen
- ⅓ of an avocado
- 1 serving chocolate protein powder
- 1 tablespoon dark cacao powder
- Pinch of salt
- 1 drop peppermint essential oil (**or** several mint leaves)
- 1 cup ice

VANILLA CREAM SMOOTHIE

ingredients

- 1 cup vanilla almond milk **or** unsweetened coconut milk
- 1 serving of vanilla protein powder
- 1 serving unflavored collagen
- ¼ cup vanilla dairy free yogurt (I love Kite Hill or So Delicious unsweetened vanilla)
- 1 tablespoon almond butter **or** tahini
- 1 serving psyllium fiber
- ½ teaspoon vanilla extract
- 3-4 cubes of ice, more for a thicker shake

Helpful Tip:

If you aren't feeling full for 3 - 4 hours after drinking a smoothie, try adding an extra scoop of protein the next day.

WILD BLUEBERRY PIE SMOOTHIE

ingredients

- ½ cup frozen organic wild blueberries
- Juice from 1 lemon
- 1 cup spinach
- 1 serving of vanilla protein powder
- ⅓ avocado (fresh or frozen)
- 2 tablespoons of seeds, such as flax, sunflower, or pumpkin
- Almond **or** coconut milk and ice to your preferred thickness

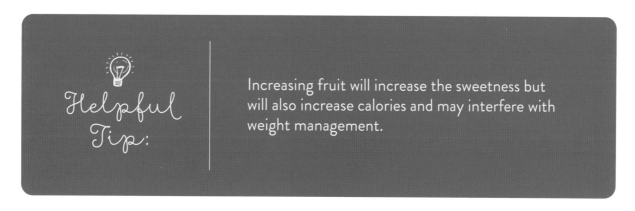

Helpful Tip:

Increasing fruit will increase the sweetness but will also increase calories and may interfere with weight management.

TROPICAL DREAMING SMOOTHIE

ingredients

- Juice from 1 orange
- 1 cup water **or** unsweetened coconut milk 3-4 cubes of ice, more for a thicker shake
- 1 cup spinach
- 1 serving of vanilla protein powder **or** 1 heaping serving collagen
- 1 scoop of chia seeds
- 1 tablespoon flaxseed oil
- ¼ cup mango / pineapple / papaya / dragonfruit

Pro Tip:

Add unlimited amounts of vegetables. Smoothies are a great way to get a few servings of vegetables in. If you're a newbie, start with less and add as you adjust to the change in taste.

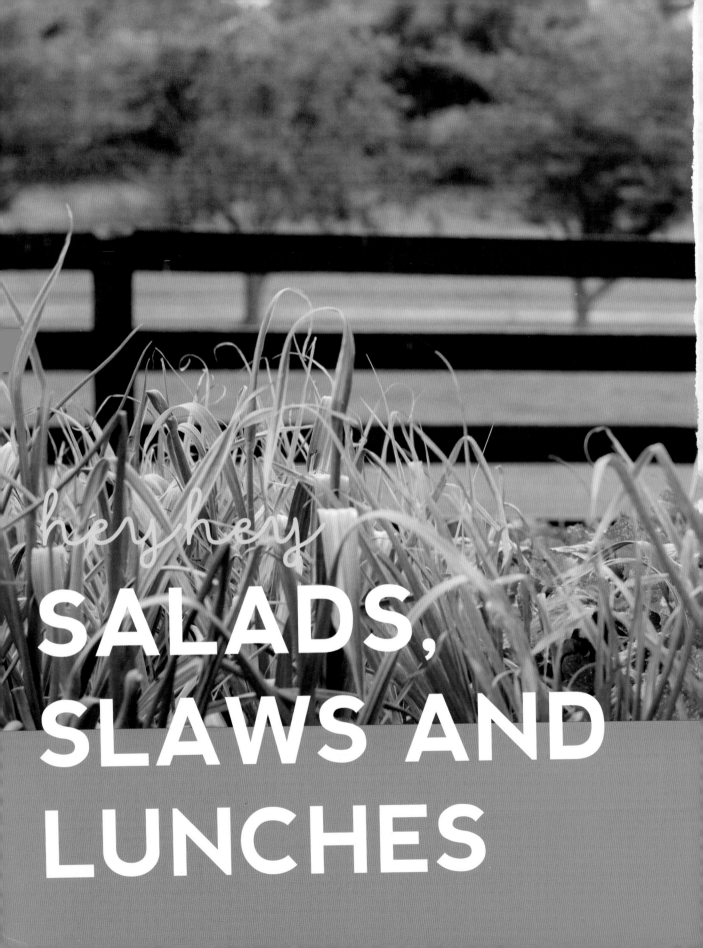

hey hey

SALADS, SLAWS AND LUNCHES

SOUTHERN CHICKEN SALAD

Serves: 4 • Prep Time: 15 minutes • Cook Time: 15 minutes

● **PALEO** ● GRAIN-FREE

ingredients

- 2 cups chopped chicken breast
- 1 cup red grapes, halved
- 2 stalks celery, diced **or** sliced
- ½ cup mayonnaise
- 1 tablespoon yellow mustard
- ⅓ cup toasted pecans (chopped)
- Salt and lots of pepper to taste

  Optional: 1 tablespoon green onion

instructions:

Assemble and stir. Amazing the next day over a bed of greens or crackers.

TIP: Poach extra chicken, while making another meal earlier in the week or grab a quality rotisserie chicken.

MAMA'S CURRY CHICKEN SALAD

Serves: 4 • Prep Time: 15 minutes • Cook Time: 15 minutes

● **PALEO** ● **GRAIN-FREE**

ingredients

- 2 cups chopped chicken breast (poached earlier in the week with another meal)
- ¼ cup diced red onion
- 1 diced apple
- 3 tablespoons yellow mustard
- ½ cup mayonnaise
- ⅓ cup toasted pecans (chopped)
- 2 tablespoons raisins, or half a kid's snack raisin box
- 3-4 tablespoons curry powder
- Salt and lots of pepper to taste

Optional: ¼ cup diced celery

instructions:

Assemble and stir. Amazing the next day over a bed of greens or crackers.

WEEKDAY TUNA SALAD

Serves: 1 • Prep Time: 5 minutes

● **PALEO**   ● GRAIN-FREE

ingredients

- 1 6-ounce can albacore tuna in water
- 1-2 teaspoons red onion, finely chopped
- 1 teaspoon capers, chopped
- 1 teaspoon dill weed (optional)
- 1 tablespoon freshly squeezed lemon juice
- 3 tablespoons olive oil
- 1 celery stick, finely sliced
- Lettuce leaves, Granny Smith or Honeycrisp, thinly sliced.

instructions:

Mix all ingredients thoroughly and serve on lettuce and slices of apple.

CHICKEN, TUNA, OR WILD CAUGHT SALMON SALAD ROLL-UPS

Serves: 1 • Prep Time: 10 minutes

● GRAIN-FREE

ingredients

- 1 can tuna, 1 cooked breast chicken or 1 can wild caught salmon cut into small pieces or mashed
- 1 celery stalk chopped in fine pieces
- 2 baby dill **or** sweet gherkin pickle chopped finely
- 1 tablespoon finely chopped onion or green onion
- 1 tablespoon mayonnaise
- Salt and pepper to taste

Optional: ½ teaspoon dill weed is great in the fish versions

instructions:

Serve the salad on leaf lettuce or a chard leaf and roll up. I also love this in a couple bibb lettuce leaves as a salad cup.

Helpful Tip:

You can also used leftover, baked salmon.

I like dill gherkins with fish and sweet gherkins with chicken.

PENNY'S DEVILED EGGS

Serves: 24 deviled eggs • Prep Time: 25 minutes • Cook Time: 10 minutes

● PALEO ● GRAIN-FREE ● **NUTRIENT DENSE**

ingredients

- 1 dozen eggs, hard boiled and sliced in half
- Filling:
  - Egg yellows, removed and mashed
  - ½ cup mayonnaise
  - 1 teaspoon honey
  - 1 teaspoon mustard
  - 1 teaspoon apple cider vinegar
  - 4 dashes hot sauce, to taste
  - White pepper to taste
  - Pinch salt to taste

instructions:

1. Hard boil eggs, chill. Slice eggs in half lengthwise, removing yellows to a seperate bowl.
2. Smash all ingredients together to taste and desired texture. I often do this with a fork, sometimes I'll use an immersion blender in a mason jar, other times I'll use an electric mixer.
3. Using a ziplock bag as a piping tube, fill with filling, snip off the corner and pipe into egg halves.
4. Top with desired toppings.
5. Enjoy being the talk of the town.

Pro Tip:

I love topping with a slice of sweet pickle or half green olive. Sometimes I add chopped bacon. A quick google will give you a multitude of options for toppings.

BROCCOLI SALAD

Serves: 4-6 • Prep Time: 15 minutes • Cook Time: 20 minutes

● GRAIN-FREE

ingredients

- 4 cups broccoli florets
- 6 pieces of bacon cooked and crumbled
- 1 cup diced celery
- ¼ cup red onion small dice
- ¼ cup sunflower seeds
- ½ cup diced apple
- ¼ cup golden raisins

Dressing:
- ¼ cup mayonnaise
- ¼ cup olive oil
- 1 tablespoon apple cider vinegar
- 1 tablespoon honey
- 1 teaspoon mustard
- Salt and pepper to taste

instructions:

1. Blanch broccoli until bright green, put on ice.
2. Crisp bacon and crumble.
3. Combine all ingredients.
4. In a mason jar, combine dressing ingredients. Shake to combine.
5. Pour dressing over salad mix. Toss to combine.
6. Serve immediately or store in refrigerator to let combine before serving.

Stores well in the refrigerator for up to 5 days.

DECONSTRUCTED GUACAMOLE SALAD

Serves: 4-6 • Prep Time: 20 minutes

● **PALEO** ● GRAIN-FREE ● **GUT HEALTH**

ingredients

- 2 cups mixed greens
- ½ cup tomato, chopped
- ½ cup jicama, chopped
- ½ cup avocado, chopped
- 1 carrot, shredded
- 2 tablespoons olive, walnut, **or** macadamia oil
- 1 lime, juiced
- ½-1 cup chopped cilantro
- Salt and pepper to taste

instructions:

Combine and toss all ingredients in a bowl and serve.

PEACH, BASIL AND ONION SALAD

Serves: 1 • Prep Time: 5 minutes

● **PALEO** ● GRAIN-FREE

ingredients

- 1 peach, sliced
- ¼ red onion, very thinly sliced
- ⅓ cup fresh basil, chopped
- ½ lemon, juiced
- 1-2 tablespoons olive oil
- Salt and pepper to taste

instructions:

Toss peach with onion, basil, lemon juice, salt and pepper. Drizzle with olive oil. Can be served over spinach or topped with chicken or fish.

STIR FRY LETTUCE WRAPS

Serves: 1 • Prep Time: 3 minutes • Cook Time: 5-8 minutes

● **PALEO** ● GRAIN-FREE

ingredients

- Leftover cooked chicken
- 1 tablespoon avocado **or** coconut oil
- Carrots, shredded
- Cabbage, shredded
- Water chestnuts, diced
- Broccoli and stalks, cut small
- Mushrooms, diced
- (Any variety of vegetable you prefer in lettuce wraps)
- 1 tablespoon coconut aminos
- 1 tablespoon sesame oil
- ¼ teaspoon salt
- Iceberg or bibb lettuce leaves
- Bean sprouts

instructions:

1. Dice small or grate: carrots, celery, broccoli stalks, mushrooms, or any variety of vegetable that you prefer.
2. Heat pan over medium-high heat.
3. Add avocado oil.
4. Add in your preferred veggies and leftover chicken for a few minutes until hot, but veggies are still crisp.
5. Add coconut aminos, sesame oil, and sea salt to your liking.
6. Scoop into fresh, washed lettuce leaves of your choice.
7. Top with fresh bean sprouts. Enjoy!

Helpful Tip:

- These are so easy to multiply and make a lovely weeknight quick dinner with precooked chicken. Served with coconut rice makes for a quick, warm dinner.
- I love to add fresh garlic and tahini to the sauce. I also love to drizzle these with the garlic tahini dressing.

TOMATO AND ONION SALAD

● **PALEO** ● **GRAIN-FREE**

ingredients

- Heirloom Tomatoes, thick sliced
- Red Onion, thinly sliced

instructions:

Combine with Mason Jar Vinaigrette (page 171) and marinate at least 15 minutes at room temperature before serving.

This is a great summer side, a wonderful base for any of the chicken salads or a nice summer snack.

SUMMER ZUCCHINI SALAD

Serves: 4-6 • Prep Time: 15 minutes

● **PALEO** ● **GRAIN-FREE**

ingredients

- 3 spiralized zucchini
- 1 bunch basil, chopped
- ⅓ cup pine nuts
- ⅓ cup golden raisins
- 2 tablespoons olive oil to taste
- 1-2 tablespoon apple cider vinegar to taste

instructions:

1. Mix all ingredients together and serve.
2. Serve chilled.

PUTTANESCA SALAD

Serves: 4 • Prep Time: 15 minutes

● **PALEO** ● GRAIN-FREE

ingredients

- 4 vine-ripened tomatoes seeded and chopped **or** 2 cups cherry tomatoes, diced
- ½ red onion, chopped
- 3 tablespoons capers
- ½ cup kalamata olives, pitted and coarsely chopped
- 6 anchovies, chopped **or** 1 teaspoon anchovy paste
- 1 garlic clove, minced
- ⅓ cup Italian **or** flat leaf parsley, coarsely chopped
- Olive oil for drizzling
- 12 fresh basil leaves, pile and roll into log to shred or tear
- Salt and black pepper

instructions:

1. Combine first seven ingredients in a medium bowl.
2. Drizzle just enough olive oil to lightly coat salad, approximately 1-2 tablespoons.
3. Sprinkle in basil, salt and pepper and toss again to mix thoroughly. Adjust seasoning to taste.

I love to serve this warm or with crisped prosciutto. This makes a wonderful topping to simple lettuce with grilled chicken the next day, too.

JICAMA SALAD

Serves: 4-6 • Prep Time: 20 minutes

● **PALEO** ● GRAIN-FREE ● **GUT HEALTH**

ingredients

- 2 grapefruits
- 2 avocados
- 1 medium sized jicama, peeled
- 1 tablespoon olive oil
- 1 jalapeño, thinly sliced
- 2 tablespoons coriander seed
- ⅓ cup olive oil
- Juice of one lime
- ¼ cup fresh cilantro leaves
- Pumpkin seeds, I prefer roasted, sprouted and salted

instructions:

1. Toast the coriander seeds and sliced jalapeño in a sauté pan with 1 tablespoon of olive oil, season well with salt and pepper and set aside to cool.
2. Cut the jicama into small sticks or thin slices about the size of a quarter.
3. Remove the peel and all of the white membrane from the grapefruit and remove the sections, place into a bowl along with the juice.
4. Add the jicama, the extra virgin olive oil and the lime juice, along with the cilantro leaves.
5. Season to taste with salt and pepper.
6. Just before serving, add the sliced avocado and gently combine.

BEET SALAD

Serves: 4-6 • Prep Time: 20 minutes

● **PALEO** ● GRAIN-FREE ● **GUT HEALTH**

ingredients

- 1 pound of beets, peeled and grated
- 4 celery sticks, finely chopped
- 1 shallot, finely chopped
- 2 tablespoons fresh mint, chopped **or** 2 tablespoons parsley **or** remove herbs and serve over 1-3 cups arugula **or** watercress
- 1 tablespoons apple cider vinegar
- 3 tablespoons olive oil
- Salt and pepper to taste

instructions:

1. In a salad bowl, toss all vegetables.
2. In a small mason jar, shake together the apple cider vinegar and olive oil and drizzle over the vegetables.
3. Add salt and pepper to taste.

PURPLE CABBAGE SUMMER SALAD

Serves: 4-6 • Prep Time: 15 minutes

● **PALEO** ● **GRAIN-FREE**

ingredients

- ½ head purple cabbage, shredded
- ½ red onion, sliced thinly
- ½ cucumber, sliced thinly
- 1 avocado, diced
- 1 medium tomato, coarsely chopped
- 1 lime, juiced
- 1-2 tablespoons olive oil
- Salt and pepper to taste

instructions:

Toss all ingredients and serve.

SUNSHINE JELLO SALAD

Serves: 9 • Prep Time: 8 minutes • Cook Time: 10 minutes

● **PALEO** ● GRAIN-FREE ● **GUT HEALTH**

ingredients

- 2 tablespoons lemon juice
- 2 cups pineapple juice
- 2 tablespoons gelatin
- 1 tablespoon white vinegar
- ¼ teaspoon salt
- 1 can crushed pineapple, juice reserved
- 1 cup carrot, shredded
- ¼ cup chopped pecans

instructions:

1. Bring juice to a low simmer.
2. Slowly whisk in gelatin.
3. Add vinegar and salt. Remove from heat.
4. Fold in pineapple, carrot and pecan pieces.
5. Pour into an 8 by 8-inch baking dish or container of choice.

Helpful Tip:

This also works great in a half sheet pan. When I make it this way, in the thinner format, I add an additional 2 teaspoons gelatin to give it more form.

EGG SALAD

● **PALEO** ● **GRAIN-FREE** ● **NUTRIENT DENSE**

ingredients

- 6 hard boiled eggs
- ½ cup mayonnaise
- 1 tablespoon dijon mustard
- 1 celery stalk, minced (optional)
- 1 baby gherkin, chopped (optional)
- ½ teaspoon salt
- ¼ teaspoon white pepper

instructions:

1. Diced the hard boiled eggs in a bowl.
2. Add all ingredients and mix well.
3. Serve on toast, crackers, with tortilla chips or in lettuce leaves.

GREEK SALAD

● **PALEO** ● GRAIN-FREE

ingredients

- Any type of loose leaf lettuce, dandelion greens, radish greens, beet greens, romaine, etc. **or** combination of greens.
- Green onion, sliced
- Roasted red peppers
- Cucumbers, sliced
- Red onion, thinly sliced
- Tomatoes, chopped
- Kalamata olives, pitted

instructions:

Add ingredients into salad bowl and liberally shake on greek salad dressing.

SUNSHINE FENNEL SLAW

Serves: 4-6 • Prep Time: 25 minutes

● **PALEO** ● GRAIN-FREE

ingredients

- 2 cups fennel, sliced thin
- 3 cups green and/or purple cabbage sliced thin
- 2 navel oranges **or** 4 mandarin oranges, peeled, segmented and chopped
- ¼ cup fresh dill chopped **or** 3 tablespoons dried dill
- 3 tablespoons extra virgin olive oil
- 2 tablespoons fresh lemon juice **or** apple cider vinegar
- ½ teaspoon quality sea salt
- ¼ teaspoon ground pepper

instructions:

1. Combine the fennel, cabbages and orange pieces in a large serving bowl. Toss.
2. In a mason jar, combine olive oil, vinegar, dill, salt and pepper. Shake to combine.
3. Pour dressing over salad mix. Toss to combine.
4. Serve immediately or store in refrigerator to let the slaw combine before serving.

Stores well in the refrigerator for up to 5 days.

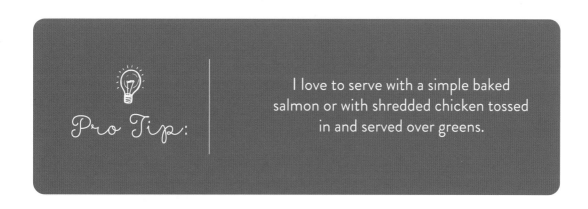

Pro Tip: I love to serve with a simple baked salmon or with shredded chicken tossed in and served over greens.

SUMMER COLESLAW

Serves: 4-6 • Prep Time: 20 minutes

● **PALEO** ● **GRAIN-FREE**

ingredients

- 1 cup shredded red cabbage
- 1 cup shredded green cabbage
- 2 carrots, shredded
- ¼ cup red onion, finely chopped
- 1 lemon, juiced
- 1 teaspoon salt
- 1 garlic clove, minced
- 1 teaspoon paprika **or** basil if nightshade free
- ⅓ cup olive oil
- 3 tablespoons apple cider vinegar
- 1 tomato, diced (optional)

instructions:

Mix all ingredients together in a large bowl and serve.

GREEK LETTUCE WRAPS

Serves: 1 • Prep Time: 15 minutes

● **PALEO** ● **GRAIN-FREE**

ingredients

- Tomatoes
- Cucumbers
- Onions
- Smashed garlic
- Extra virgin olive oil
- Lemon juice
- Fresh basil (or other preferred herbs)
- Olives
- Lettuce leaves
- Dried oregano to sprinkle
- Sheep's feta to garnish, optional

instructions:

1. Dice small: tomatoes, cucumbers, onion, (a little smashed garlic) toss with extra virgin oil, a little lemon juice; add fresh basil chopped or any herbs that you prefer.
2. Spoon vegetables into fresh, washed lettuce leaves and add a few good olives. Roll cabbage roll style.

Helpful
Tip:

I like to serve this
as a vegetarian meal
or add in greek
marinated chicken.

hey hey

MARINADES, DRIZZLES AND DIPS

MARINADES, DRIZZLES AND DIPS

While we're making things simple, I like to think about seasoning in one of 3 ways: we marinade or rub food down before cooking, we drizzle food when we plate it up or we offer a dip with the plate. And there's the oldie, but goodie: salt and pepper well before cooking, but I didn't want to bore you with basics.

My favorite tools to use when quick mixing sauces and marinades:

- Balsamic vinegar
- Rice wine vinegar
- Apple cider vinegar
- Red wine vinegar
- Fancier, nice vinegars from specialty shops
- Coconut Aminos
- Nut Butters and nuts
- Tahini
- Citrus Juices
- Pomegranate Juice
- Dried herbs
- Salt and Pepper

CAESAR DRESSING

● **PALEO** ● **GRAIN-FREE**

ingredients

- ¼ to ⅓ cup extra virgin olive oil
- ½ teaspoon anchovy paste
- 1 teaspoon dijon style mustard
- 1 minced clove of garlic
- ⅛ teaspoon gluten free worcestershire sauce
- ¼ teaspoon ground pepper
  (I prefer white pepper!)
- 1 tablespoon lemon juice

instructions:

Combine all ingredients in mason jar and immersion blend or whisk until smooth. Makes a great marinade for chicken, too.

RUBS

● **PALEO** ● **GRAIN-FREE**

instructions:

1. Mix well and rub onto meat.
2. Bake, broil or grill as desired. After baking fish, sprinkle with lemon juice.

CHICKEN RUB

ingredients

- ½ teaspoon sea salt
- ½ teaspoon rosemary - crushed
- ¼ teaspoon paprika
- ⅛ teaspoon black pepper
- 1 teaspoon garlic powder **or** 2 tablespoons fresh garlic, minced
- ¼ teaspoon onion powder

MEDITERRANEAN MEAT AND FISH RUB

ingredients

- ½ teaspoon salt
- ⅛ teaspoon curry powder
- ¼ teaspoon paprika
- ⅛ teaspoon black pepper
- a pinch or two of ground red pepper **or** red pepper flakes
- ¼ teaspoon garlic
- ¼ teaspoon onion powder
- Fish (salmon, halibut, tilapia, etc)

DILL FISH RUB

ingredients

- ½ teaspoon salt
- ⅛ teaspoon black pepper
- ¼ teaspoon garlic powder
- 2 tablespoons dill weed
- Fish (salmon, halibut, tilapia, etc)

 **PICTURED LEFT TO RIGHT:**
Chicken, Mediterranean, Dill

SIMPLE TAHINI DRESSING

● **PALEO** ● GRAIN-FREE

instructions:

1. Mix 2 tablespoons of sesame tahini with desired amount of lemon juice to your own taste.
2. Mix a little water to thin dressing to desired consistency.

BERRY FRIDGE JAM

Serves: 1 half-pint of jam • Prep Time: 10 minutes • Cook Time: 30 minutes

● **PALEO** ● **GRAIN-FREE**

ingredients

- 10 ounce bag of frozen fruit of choice
- 1 tablespoon monk fruit sweetener **or** 2 tablespoons honey
- 1 tablespoon pure lemon juice
- 2 tablespoons chia seeds **or** 2 tablespoons arrowroot powder
  (dissolved in 2 tbsp of water before incorporating)

instructions:

1. Combine fruit, sweetener and lemon juice in a pot over medium-low heat and allow to simmer. Stir frequently and smash berries down.
2. As the sauce begins to reduce, slowly add arrowroot powder or chia into mixture, allowing to incorporate and thicken before adding more. Stop adding arrowroot powder just before desired thickness occurs.
3. As the jam simmers it will thicken even more. You may enjoy the jam warm, and allow to cool and store in refrigerator.

This is so yummy when you have ripe summer fruits and offers a great sweet option. We love peaches, blueberries, cranberries (especially if you love tart flavors), and cherries! You can use organic frozen fruit too!

Swirl a spoon into cashew or coconut yogurt, top with chia seeds and pumpkin or sunflower seed for a little added crunch!

Helpful Tip:

A mason jar is perfect storage for this jam. I also love to make this jam from cranberries around the holidays, though I do double the sweetener to compensate for the tart cranberries.

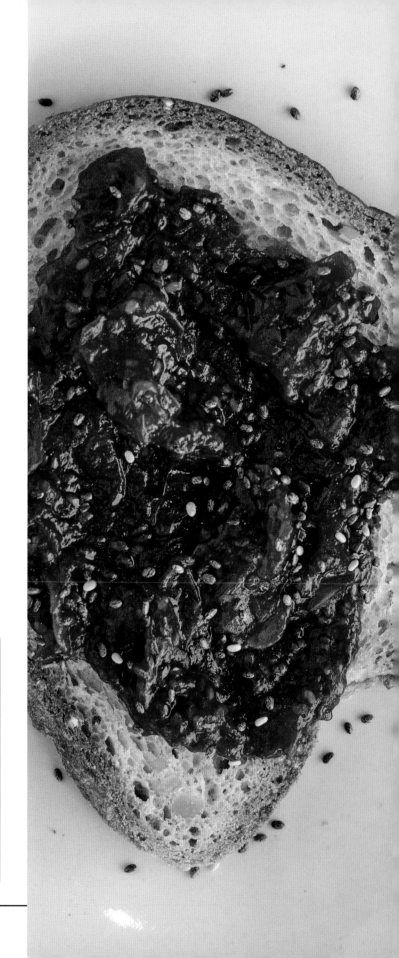

SLOW COOKER MARINADE

● **PALEO** ● GRAIN-FREE

ingredients

- ⅓ cup coconut aminos
- ¼ cup gluten free worcestershire
- 2-4 cloves garlic, minced
- 2 tablespoons italian seasoning
- 2 lemons, juiced
- ¼ cup avocado oil
- Salt and pepper to taste

instructions:

Combine all ingredients, pour over meat in slow cooker or instapot. If more liquid is needed for cooking, I like to use beef or chicken stock. Can also be used as a yummy marinade for grilled meats, too.

EASIEST MAYO

Serves: 1 ½ cups • Prep Time: 5 minutes

● PALEO ● GRAIN-FREE ● **NUTRIENT DENSE**

Here she is: your gateway drug. A weekly mayo creation will be the vehicle for all of your favorite dips and dressings that change the weeknight eating game. This is so simple, my youngest whips it up with a bit of supervision over that immersion blender use. And I know what you're thinking: another kitchen appliance just for a dip? Yes. I strive to keep my kitchen minimal, but a quality immersion blender kept in a handy drawer will uplevel your dressing and seasoning game. Heck - I even mix guac in a mason jar with the immersion blender instead of mashing it with my fork. The bottom blade portion detaches and comes clean quickly with a hot water rinse.

ingredients

- 1 large egg (at room temperature)
- 1 teaspoon Dijon mustard
- 2 teaspoons apple cider vinegar (**or** white vinegar if not paleo)
- ¼ teaspoon sea salt (**or** ½ tsp if you like saltier mayo)
- 1 cup avocado **or** olive oil
- **TIP:** Once done, you can stir in a variety of add ins:
  - Fresh garlic for garlic mayo
  - 1-2 tablespoons herbs de provence for herb mayo spread or a dip
  - Taco seasoning for a fun taco topper
  - Clean sriracha for spicy sriracha aioli
  - Capers and 1-2 diced gherkins for a tartar sauce

instructions:

1. Crack egg into a tall jar or glass (large enough for an immersion blender to fit).
2. Gently add Dijon mustard, apple cider vinegar, and salt.
3. Pour oil on top. Be very careful not to disturb the egg at this point.
4. Carefully submerge the immersion blender into the bottom of the jar and blend on low power for about 20 seconds -- until you see most of the jar has turned white.
5. Slowly move the blender up and down without removing it from being submerged. Continue to move up and down until mayonnaise forms.
6. Store in refrigerator.

LINDEN HILLS SALAD DRESSING

Serves: Everyone • Prep Time: 10 minutes • Cook Time: 30 minutes

● GRAIN-FREE

This dressing is a riff on our family's favorite store bought dressing. It used to be available only near where my Mom grew up and we've done everything from drive a couple hours, to pick up a case, to shipping it straight from the company. The ingredient list is less than lovely, full of high fructose corn syrup and stabilizers, so I made a cleaner recipe. It's essentially the best French dressing you'll ever have and THE BEST dip for getting littles to nosh on raw veggies. It also makes a fabulous marinade for a grilled flank steak.

ingredients

- 1 cup avocado oil
- ½ cup honey
- 1 can tomato soup
- ½ cup vinegar
- ⅛ teaspoon garlic powder
- 1 teaspoon dry mustard
- 1 teaspoon salt
- 1 teaspoon celery seed
- ¼ teaspoon cracked black peppercorns
- ½-1 teaspoon arrowroot powder to thicken, if desired

instructions:

1. Mix all ingredients in a blender until creamy.
2. Pour into jar and keep in the fridge.

LEMON GARLIC TAHINI

Serves: 4 • Prep Time: 5 minutes

● **PALEO** ● **GRAIN-FREE**

ingredients

- ½ cup tahini
- 2-3 tablespoons lemon juice
- ½ cup water
- 3 cloves of garlic
- 1 teaspoon sea salt
- 2 tablespoons olive oil
- Optional: 3 tablespoons honey

instructions:

Combine all ingredients in mason jar and immersion blend until smooth.

Use as salad dressing, dress your roasted veggies, serve as a dip for veggies or drizzle anywhere you need a little flavor boost.

SIMPLE SALSA

Serves: 4 • Prep Time: 15 minutes

● PALEO ● GRAIN-FREE

ingredients

- 2 large diced tomatoes **or** 1 cup cherry tomatoes, diced
- 2 scallions, thinly chopped
- 1 garlic clove, minced
- 1 tablespoon chopped cilantro (fresh is best)
- 1 tablespoon organic extra virgin olive oil
- 2 teaspoons fresh lime juice

instructions:

Combine all ingredients in a bowl and let sit a few minutes before serving. This is great as a topping on fish.

MOROCCAN RELISH

Serves: 4 • Prep Time: 5 minutes

● **PALEO** ● **GRAIN-FREE**

ingredients

- ¾ cup extra virgin olive oil
- 1 tablespoon fresh lemon juice
- 1 tablespoon fresh lime juice
- 1 tablespoon ground coriander
- 1 tablespoon ground cumin
- 1 teaspoon sweet or smoked paprika
- ¼ cup fresh cilantro, minced
- 4 large cloves garlic, minced
- 1 teaspoon red pepper flakes
- 1 shallot, halved and thinly sliced
- Sea salt to taste

instructions:

1. Combine ingredients in a medium bowl and season with salt. For a smoother consistency, puree in a food processor or use your immersion blender in a mason jar.
2. Cover and let sit at least 1 hour at room temperature to let flavors meld. Sauce will keep, covered and refrigerated, for up to 4 days.

Use this relish to dress cooked vegetables or as a marinade for fish.

MASON JAR VINAIGRETTE

This recipe is my favorite of all time. You can make it any old time, just grab a mason jar, pour everything in and shake it up real quick.

● **PALEO** ● **GRAIN-FREE**

ingredients

- ½ cup extra virgin olive oil
- 3 tablespoons apple cider vinegar
- 1 teaspoon dried oregano **or** other fresh herbs to compliment your meal
- ½ teaspoon salt
- ⅛ teaspoon pepper

instructions:

Mix this in a container and refrigerate ahead of time. Just let it sit out a few minutes before using.

HEY HEY RANCH

Serves: 4 • Prep Time: 5 minutes

● **PALEO** ● GRAIN-FREE

ingredients

- ½ cup mayonnaise
- ⅓ cup coconut milk
- 1 teaspoon parsley
- ½ teaspoon dill
- ½ teaspoon garlic powder
- ½ teaspoon onion powder
- ½ teaspoon chives
- ¼ teaspoon salt
- ¼ teaspoon black pepper

instructions:

Combine all ingredients in a mason jar and immersion blend until smooth.

TIP: Combining just the dry components of this ranch dressing make for a fabulous rub. I typically add more salt to season the meat more and 3x or 4x the other ingredients.

MUSTARD AND OLIVE OIL DRESSING

Serves: 4 • Prep Time: 5 minutes

● GRAIN-FREE

ingredients

- ½ cup extra virgin olive oil
- 6 tablespoons balsamic vinegar or lemon juice
- 4 tablespoons water
- 1 teaspoon dijon mustard
- ⅛ teaspoon oregano
- Salt and Pepper to taste
- 1 minced garlic clove
- Optional: Add 3 tablespoons honey

instructions:

Combine all ingredients into a mason jar, shake to blend. If you decide to add a bit of honey, I won't tell and you'll have a lovely little honey mustard sauce. When I do this, I use a bit less than 2 tablespoons water, then choose lemon juice over balsamic vinegar to keep the sweetness of one variety.

hey hey
VEGETABLES

ROASTED OKRA

Serves: 4-6 • Prep Time: 10 minutes • Cook Time: 20 minutes

● **PALEO** ● GRAIN-FREE ● **GUT HEALTH**

ingredients

- 1 pound of okra
- 2-3 tablespoons of healthy fat (bacon grease, lard, **or** avocado oil)
- 3-5 tablespoons cumin **and/or** coriander
- Salt to taste

instructions:

1. Cut off tops and slice lengthwise for a fry experience or widthwise for bite-sized poppers.
2. Toss with fat of choice, melted.
3. Add cumin and coriander and salt.
4. Toss in 425°F oven either on a baking sheet lined with a rack or parchment paper.
5. Roast 10 - 20 min until browning and crisp.

Helpful Tips:

• Serve as a snack or quick lunch - roasted okra & salami with Snyder's of Hanover gluten free pretzel sticks is so yummy and quick.

• Frozen okra works great for this, too. I like to pop them in the oven without seasoning to thaw and allow the frozen liquid to disperse. Remove from sheet pan for a quick toss in fat and seasonings, then back to the oven for roasting.

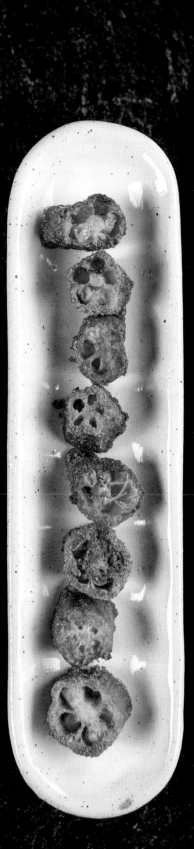
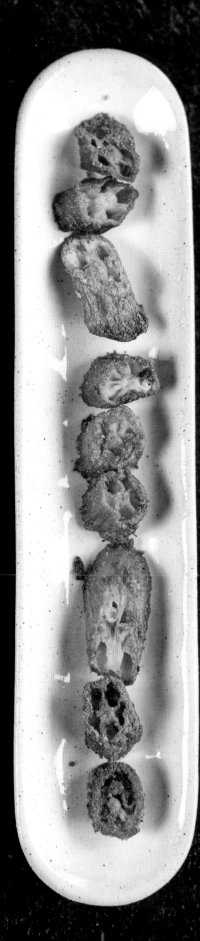

STEAMED BROCCOLI

● PALEO ● GRAIN-FREE

instructions:

1. Rinse thoroughly. You may want to soak in salted water for 5 minutes, then rinse thoroughly.
2. Cut up to fit in steamer or large pan with boiling water.
3. Steam for about 4-5 minutes till slightly tender. Do Not Overcook. When broccoli turns bright green, you're nearly done. You may sprinkle with lemon juice or sauté with garlic and oil – only steam broccoli for 2 minutes if opting to saute, next.

GARLIC-CHILI ROASTED BROCCOLI

● PALEO ● GRAIN-FREE

ingredients

- ¼ cup olive oil
- 6 cloves garlic, finely chopped
- 1 tablespoon chili powder
- 1 tablespoon seasoned salt
- 1 large head of broccoli, cut into thin long spears

instructions:

1. Preheat oven to 425°F.
2. Place olive oil, garlic, chili powder and seasoned salt in the bottom of a large bowl and add the broccoli spears. Coat evenly and place on a large baking sheet.
3. Roast broccoli until ends are crisp and brown and stalks are just tender, approximately 15 minutes.

MARINATED ASPARAGUS SALAD

● GRAIN-FREE ● GUT HEALTH

ingredients

- 2 pounds asparagus
- 2 small shallots diced
- 1 red or yellow pepper, finely chopped (optional)
- 1 stalk celery, finely chopped

Marinade:
- ¾ avocado oil
- ½ cup red wine vinegar
- ⅓ cup honey or balsamic vinegar
- ½ clove garlic, minced
- ¼ teaspoon paprika

instructions:

1. Rinse and cut bottom part of stalk (it is too fibrous). If you hold each end of the asparagus and bend, the plant will naturally snap above the more fibrous portion.
2. Blanch asparagus, immediately chill in ice water.
3. Place in 13 by 9-inch baking dish.
4. Mix marinade well.
5. Pour over vegetables.
6. Chill 4 hours or overnight.

I keep these handy in the fridge and grab a few spears for a quick, veggie snack.

ROASTED ASPARAGUS

● PALEO   ● GRAIN-FREE   ● GUT HEALTH

instructions:

1. Rinse and cut bottom part of stalk (it is too fibrous). If you hold each end of the asparagus and bend, the plant will naturally snap above the more fibrous portion.

When Roasting (pictured):
- When roasting in the oven, toss with olive oil and butter, line up on a baking sheet, cover with 2-5 tablespoons minced garlic, salt and pepper. Roast at 425°F to texture of your choosing.

When Steaming:
- Bring ¼ inch of water to a boil in a large pan.
- Steam asparagus in the water for 3 minutes only. Rinse with cold water. The asparagus should remain slightly crisp - do not over cook. You could also blanch them for 2 minutes and sauté with garlic and olive oil or roast in the oven for a variation.

ROASTED CAULIFLOWER

● **PALEO** ● GRAIN-FREE

ingredients

- 1 head of cauliflower
- 3 tablespoons nutritional yeast
- 1-3 cloves garlic, minced **or** dusting of garlic powder
- 1 tablespoon olive oil
- Sea salt and pepper
- 1-3 tablespoons herb of your choosing; parsley, cilantro for mexi nights, bail and oregano for greek nights

instructions:

Preheat oven to 425°F. Toss cauliflower with olive oil. Spread out on a baking dish and sprinkle with nutritional yeast and sea salt. Bake 30 minutes or until tender and begins to brown.

MASHED CAULI-TATOS

● **PALEO** ● GRAIN-FREE

ingredients

- 6 cups chopped cauliflower
- ¼ cup flax oil **or** extra virgin olive oil **or** ghee
- Salt and pepper to taste

instructions:

Process cauliflower in a food processor with "S" blade, chop until "grainy". In a large pot, slow cooker, or electric skillet on the lowest temperature, add oil, spices and cauliflower, stirring and tossing until coated and warmed to 105°F. If using flax seed oil do not heat over 110°F. You may use a higher heat when using olive oil or ghee, though the flax seed oil adds a distinct nuttiness. Smash with a potato masher until you've reached desired consistency.

BRUSSELS AND BACON

● **PALEO** ● **GRAIN-FREE**

ingredients

- 1 pound of brussel sprouts, halved
- 2-6 pieces bacon, chopped
- 1 sweet onion diced
- Sea salt and pepper

instructions:

1. Preheat oven to 425°F.
2. Slice bacon, place in cast iron pan or skillet until half cooked and fat is rendering well. Add diced onion. Cook on medium low until translucent and some browning.
3. Chop brussel sprouts. Add to pan with bacon and onions. Bring heat to medium high, stirring every few minutes. Remove from heat once bright green and fork tender, 7-10 minutes.

ROASTED MAPLE BRUSSELS SPROUTS

● **GRAIN-FREE**

ingredients

- 1 pound of brussel sprouts, shredded **or** chopped thin
- 2 tablespoons Olive oil, divided
- Sea salt and pepper
- 1 teaspoon Balsamic vinegar
- 1 tablespoon Maple syrup

instructions:

1. Preheat oven to 425°F.
2. Shred or thinly chop brussel sprouts. Toss with 1 tablespoon olive oil, sea salt, & pepper.
3. Spread on a thin layer on a cookie sheet and bake until tender and crispy.
4. While baking, whisk the dressing - balsamic vinegar, maple syrup and remaining olive oil. Once brussel sprouts are finished roasting, coat with dressing. Serve warm.

SAUTEED GREEN BEANS WITH BACON

● **PALEO** ● GRAIN-FREE

ingredients

- 1 pound green beans
- 1 tablespoon bacon grease
- 2 cloves garlic, minced
- 1 tablespoon coconut aminos

instructions:

Slice green beans to desired length. Heat up bacon grease in a frying pan. Once hot, add green beans and cook for 2 -3 minutes or until they are cooked through. Add garlic and coconut aminos. Season with salt and pepper.

TIP: I love to toss these with some toasted almond slivers for depth.

SPAGHETTI SQUASH

● PALEO

ingredients

- 1 large Spaghetti squash
- Avocado **or** coconut oil
- Garlic powder to taste
- Salt and pepper to taste

instructions:

Preheat oven to 350°F. Cut spaghetti squash in half, length wise. Remove seeds. Rub inside and out with oil. Sprinkle flesh with garlic powder, salt and pepper. Place on parchment paper lined baking sheet, skin side up and bake 25-30 minutes until fork tender.

Remove from oven and shred the squash with a fork. It will look like spaghetti. Serve with primavera vegetables or marinara sauce.

KALE

● **PALEO** ● **GRAIN-FREE**

ingredients

- 1 bunch of Lacinato kale (this is a flatter, milder flavored, darker green leaf than the curly kale)
- 1 cup water for steaming
- Pinch of salt
- Minced garlic **and/or** onion
- Coconut, olive, walnut or macadamia nut oil

instructions:

Cut the kale into strips. Steam kale in salted water for 3 minutes. You may add minced garlic and onion as an option. Add a drizzle of oil an sprinkle of salt just before serving.

KALE CHIPS

● **PALEO** ● **GRAIN-FREE**

ingredients

- 6 cups chopped kale
- ¼ cup flax oil **or** extra virgin olive oil or ghee
- Salt and pepper to taste

instructions:

Preheat oven to 350°F. With your fingers, carefully remove the kale leaves from the thick stems and tear into bite-size pieces. Drizzle oil over the kale and massage it in. Spread out evenly on cookie sheet and sprinkle with sea salt. Place in oven for 10 minutes or until crispy.

PRIMAVERA VEGGIES

● **PALEO** ● **GRAIN-FREE**

ingredients

- 8-10 cups of vegetables rough chopped or sliced, made up of a mix of:
    - Mushrooms
    - Zucchini
    - Yellow Squash
    - Broccoli
    - Onion
- 2-4 cloves garlic, minced
- 1 jar clean marinara sauce like Rao's

instructions:

Toss all in a casserole dish, pour marinara sauce on top - cook in a 350°F oven until warmed through, 15-30 minutes. Serve on top of gluten free pasta or spaghetti squash.

BEETS (2-WAYS)

● GRAIN-FREE ● GUT HEALTH

STEAMED

instructions:

Wash and cut off the stems. Place beets in a pot and fill water just to where it touches the beets. Steam approximately 30 minutes for a medium beet, or longer for larger beets. Be sure to turn several times during cooking. They should be fork tender to pierce. To easily peel, drop cooked beets in an ice bath, peel skins. Serve warm, sliced or slice and refrigerate for up to 5 days.

ROASTED

instructions:

Wash and cut off the stems. Roughly dice dime-sized, toss in a little avocado oil or animal fat, roast for 15-20 mins at 425°F. I also like to add a tablespoon or two of maple syrup in the last minutes of roasting for some contrast. These are a lovely side, when sprinkled with toasted pistachios and crumbled goat cheese.

ROASTED SWEET POTATOES

● PALEO ● GRAIN-FREE

ingredients:

- 4-5 medium sweet potatoes, peeled and diced
- 2 sweet onions cut into one inch pieces
- 1 ½ tablespoons cooking fat of choice
- ¾ teaspoon minced garlic
- Several grinds of freshly ground pepper
- ½ teaspoon sea salt

instructions:

1. Preheat oven to 425°F.
2. In a large bowl combine all ingredients and toss thoroughly.
3. Spread onto 9 X 13 baking dish and bake for 30 to 35 minutes or until tender. For crispier potatoes, do not turn.

SWEET POTATO SLICES (2-WAYS)

● PALEO ● GRAIN-FREE

SWEET POTATO TOASTS

instructions:

Peel and slice potatoes. Slice lengthwise into ¼" thick slices. Place in toaster several times until desired texture or pan fry on both sides in a shallow bit of coconut oil. Use as a bread-like vehicle.

HOMEFRIES

instructions:

Peel and slice potatoes. Slice width wise into coins. Pan fry in coconut oil until browning, turn. Remove from heat.

Pro Tip:

Top with various toppings. Guac and Everything But The Bagel seasoning, sunflower butter and pomegranate seeds with cinnamon. Avocado smash, balsamic glaze, cherry tomato slices. These are a great traditional carb replacement and work as a vehicle for soooo much.

SHEET PAN VEGGIES

● **PALEO** ● GRAIN-FREE

My top tip to avoid wondering what you're going to make for dinner...prep it! I love a massive veggie prep to easily grab through the week and cook a ton of different ways. It's usually easy to make double when you're going through the trouble to make it once.

Chop up these veggies early in the week and use in meals throughout the week. Saves so much time! These veggies are versatile and can be used several ways — roasted in the oven, stir frys, soups, sheet pan dinners.

ingredients

- Purple onion
- Green pepper
- Zucchini
- Red pepper
- Mushrooms
- Carrot
- Broccoli
- Butternut squash
- Turnips
- Cabbage
- Okra
- Radishes
- Beets
- Acorn squash

instructions:

Turn your oven to 425°F. Prepare sheet pans with a parchment paper lining. Toss equally sized chopped veggies in cooking fat of choice. Lard and duck fat are my favorites for this application. Season with salt and pepper, other herbs, as desired. Spread out onto sheet pans, allowing room. Toss every 10 minutes until veggies have reached your desired texture. I like to cook the veggies I will reserve for later meals to just before complete, so that reheating can add a final crisp.

SWISS CHARD

● PALEO ● GRAIN-FREE

instructions:

1. Wash leaves thoroughly and remove stems. Cut width wise into strips.
2. Bring ½ inch of water to boil and steam for 3 minutes.
3. This has a very mild, almost spinach-like taste.
4. Top with lemon juice, salt and sunflower or pumpkin seeds, if you like.

BALSAMIC SWISS CHARD

● PALEO ● GRAIN-FREE

instructions:

1. Wash leaves of 1 bunch chard thoroughly and remove stems. Cut width wise into strips. Diced stems into ¼ inch pieces.
2. Heat cast iron skillet over medium heat. Briefly cook chard stems until color brightens, add leaves. Add 1-2 tablespoons chopped garlic and 1-2 tablespoons balsamic vinegar. Remove from heat and serve. Pistachios are a wonderful accent on top.

This preparation yields a savory, sweet flavor offsetting the chard's bitter nature.

SAUTEED SPINACH

● PALEO ● GRAIN-FREE

instructions:

1. Thoroughly wash spinach and spin dry, if fresh.
2. In frying pan add 1- 1 ½ tablespoons extra virgin olive oil.
3. 1 tablespoon grass-fed butter, if tolerated.
4. 1 - 2 minced garlic cloves.
5. Add everything into pan and sauté until spinach is just wilted.

CABBAGE, CARROTS AND ONIONS

● PALEO ● GRAIN-FREE

ingredients

- ¼ inch of water in large skillet
- Green cabbage - sliced width wise in 1 inch squares
- Sliced onion
- Diced carrots
- Optional seasoning mix to add while steaming (whole seed): mustard seeds, peppercorns, coriander, whole clove, star anise.

instructions:

1. Steam for about 5 minutes until soft.
2. Serve with a sprinkle of salt and pepper.
3. If using, you want to keep the seasoning mix away from the steamed veggies, so make use of a steamer basket or similar. Cabbage will take on the flavors it's cooked with and cabbage is nourishing for the gut. I love making this with the ranch roast.

heyhey
DINNERS

DINNERTIME

BUILDING YOUR WEEKNIGHT MEAL

While I really enjoy a thoughtful, long-reading dinner recipe, most of our dinners begin with a tired mom, starving boys and limited time. These recipes are the result of that need and a preference for living life over being stuck in my kitchen. I like to think of the week's meals as being built around a couple batches of protein, lots of veggies and a sauce or two that can be spun up a few different ways based on what it's garnished with.

You've got options:

Buddha or Taco Bowl
Tacos
Modern Meat and Three
Weeknight Pho or Simple Soup
Sheet Pan Dinner

THOUGHTS ON COOKING MEAT

As a kid I was not a fan of meat, partially because I didn't digest it and partially because of the texture. And then I became an adult who didn't love meat for the same reasons. As I began to heal and digested, even craved meat - cooking it was still a struggle for me.

Since then - I've learned to employ some simple tactics that make quality meat shine and make the process enjoyable. The key to yummy meat meals is quality, pastured meat - chicken that tastes like chicken, for example - this is where meat shines.

Having a hot cast iron pan for cooking meat from room temp, ample seasoning or marinating before cooking and a willingness to sear everything before it goes in the instapot are my foundations.

How you think matters here, too. When I adopted the attitude that meat could be really simple and veggies could be the star of the show, the game changed for me.

A simple Grass-fed steak or pastured pork chop, seasoned with salt and pepper and a single herb before hitting a hot cast iron pan creates a crispy savory crust. Once searing is complete you can easily pop the cast iron in the oven until you use your hand dandy secret weapon - the thermometer.

From there it's just a science experiment until the thermometer meets the desired temperature. This works just the same on your grill. The below is a rough guide, you can, of course cook meats like beef to a more well done temp or enjoy them a bit more rare, within your comfort level. I will note that I love a pastured pork chop to a lower temp then we're used to cooking grocery pork.

165°F – All poultry, wild game
160°F – Ground meat and ground meat mixes
145°F – Fresh beef, pork, veal, lamb and fish

WHAT IS A BUDDHA BOWL?

It's God's gift to weeknight cooks, really...this is how we eat most of our meals. They are nutrient dense, simple, and can be customized to any flavor - from taco bowl to mediterranean bowl and everything in between. With a focus on building the ideal plate of healthy fat, fiber, protein, vegetables, and fermented food to nourish and keep blood sugar balanced, bowls are easy peasy. They're also great to customize for a household mix of heavy grain-eating teens, a lower-carb focused parent and the kid who sprays rice around the room, and thus doesn't get much opportunity with grains.

I like to keep this really simple, focusing on something that can be easily assembled in minutes after the prep work has been done. I often cook our meats and veggies for more than just one meal, so we can cook once and eat a few meals from it. If you're cooking once, there's usually not much more effort needed to cook more.

one

START WITH A BASE

Start with your base, loose leafy greens are a great bottom.

- Chopped Kale
- Spinach
- Arugula
- Romaine Lettuce
- Shredded cabbage or slaw mix
- Watercress
- Cauliflower rice
- Coconut rice
- Brown Rice
- Bone broth

two

ADD THAT PROTEIN!

Step 2: Add one or a few, but don't skip the protein!

- Roasted / shredded / rotisserie grilled chicken
- Pork carnitas
- Ground pork
- Beef
- Bacon
- Hard boiled eggs
- Fish
- Shrimp
- Scallops
- Tuna salad
- Chicken salad
- Smoked turkey
- Ground taco turkey, beef or ancestral blend
- Lamb

three

ADD SOME VEGGIES (FIBER!)

- Roasted carrots
- Bok choy
- Broccoli
- Cooked greens
- Diced celery
- Roasted or pickled beets
- Fresh or shredded carrots
- Cauliflower
- Brussels sprouts
- Artichokes
- Peas
- Cucumber
- Tomato
- Mushrooms
- Squash
- Peppers
- Riced cauliflower

four

ADD FAT

- Avocado
- Olives
- Nuts
- Seeds
- Salad dressing, dip or drizzle
- Pesto

five

ADD A LITTLE FERMENTED SIDE

- Favorite krauts (I love Wildbrine Raw Organic Sauerkraut)
- Fermented pickles (I love Bubbie's dill pickles)
- Fermented yogurt like Culina Yogurt or Cocoyo Yogurt (can be used as substitutes for sour cream)
- Kimchi (Wildbrine or other)
- Fermented hot sauces (Wildbrine or local)
- Fermented or pickled beets
- Fermented carrots
- Fermented giardiniera

six

TAKE A TRIP TO FLAVORTOWN

Top it with a sauce and fresh herbs if you have them.

- Sliced green onions
- Chiffonade basil
- Chopped cilantro
- Rosemary
- Sliced jalapenos
- Fresh herbs

seven

OPTIONAL

- **Grains:** organic brown rice, wild rice, quinoa, amaranth

  TIP: Grains are best for our bodies and easiest on our digestion when they have been soaked and sprouted before cooking. This predigests difficult portions of grains and helps to remove antinutrients or toxic components.

  TIP: Best if cooked in a nutrient dense way, such as cooking in bone broth instead of water.

  TIP: I also like to cook coconut rice: instead of using water or bone broth I will add 1 part coconut milk or cream to 1 part bone broth or water to make up the total cooking liquid.

- **Beans and legumes:** black beans, chickpeas, lentils, hummus
- **Fruit:** fresh, dried and freeze dried: berries, dried apples, apple slices, peach slices, pear slices
- **Cheese....**Dear Americans, We need to talk. Cheese is a condiment, not an entire meal. If you are in a healing phase, it may be best to eliminate dairy altogether. If you are in a maintenance phase, use a little quality cheese sparingly. Ok?

BOWL CONCEPTS

TACO BOWL

- Base: romaine / mixed greens / kale / arugula
- Protein: taco meat / pulled chicken / grilled steak
- Veggies, Fiber: roasted red peppers / corn / tomatoes / shredded cabbage / onions and peppers / guacamole / jicama
- Fat: avocado / sunflower seeds
- Fermented: kimchi, fermented jalapenos or fermented hot sauce
- Grains/Legumes: coconut rice / quinoa / brown rice / black beans
- Top with: cilantro / salsa / lime cilantro vinaigrette / hot sauce

Mix all ingredients together in a large bowl and serve.

MEDITTERANEAN BOWL

- Base: romaine / arugula / leaf lettuce / kale
- Protein: roasted chicken / salmon / grilled steak
- Veggies, Fiber: tomatoes / bell peppers / red onion / roasted sumac cauliflower / roasted broccoli
- Fat: avocado, tahini, slivered almonds, olive oil drizzle, olives
- Fermented: pickled onions, beet kraut
- Grains/Legumes: brown rice / quinoa / lentils
- Top with: tahini dressing / hummus / garlic sauce / sheeps feta

EARTHY BOWL

- Base: shredded kale / arugula / cooked collard greens / cauliflower rice / mashed cauliflower
- Protein: shredded chicken / pulled pork
- Veggies, Fiber: sauteed portobellos / shredded beets / cucumbers / squash
- Fat: Avocado / raw pumpkin seeds
- Fermented: beet kraut / fermented hot sauce
- Grains/Legumes: wild rice / quinoa / lentils
- Top with: basil / lemon garlic tahini dressing

HARVEST BOWL

- Base: shredded kale
- Protein: roasted chicken
- Veggies, Fiber: roasted sweet potatoes / apples / roasted butternut squash / brussels and bacon
- Fat: sliced almonds / roasted pumpkin seeds / sunflower seeds
- Fermented: traditional saurkraut
- Grains/Legumes: warm quinoa / black eyed peas / roasted chickpas
- Top with: goat cheese / balsamic vinaigrette

Mix all ingredients together in a large bowl and serve.

PESTO BOWL

- Base: warm sauteed kale / cooked collards / romaine
- Protein: chicken / turkey meatballs / breakfast meatloaves
- Veggies, Fiber: zucchini / zoodles / eggplant / roasted cauliflower / marinara
- Fat: pesto sauce / garlic olive oil drizzle
- Fermented: fermented yogurt drizzle or dip
- Grains/Legumes: quinoa
- Top with: pesto sauce

POKE BOWL

- Base: shredded kale or brussels / white or brown rice / coconut rice
- Protein: miso salmon or spicy tuna or grilled shrimp
- Veggies, Fiber: shredded carrots / kelp / seaweed / cucumber / radish / lime / shredded cabbage / green onions
- Fat: avocado / sesame seeds / tahini
- Fermented: fermented jalapenos or pickled jalapenos
- Grains/Legumes: brown rice / coconut rice
- Top with: furikake / sesame seeds / spicy sriracha aioli / coconut aminos / ginger / wasabi / mango

BALSAMIC CHICKEN THIGHS

- Base: cooked collards / shredded kale or brussels / shredded napa cabbage
- Protein: balsamic chicken thighs / pulled pork
- Veggies, Fiber: roasted carrots / roasted butternut squash broccoli
- Fat: pumpkin seeds / sunflower seeds
- Fermented: beet kraut
- Grains/Legumes: coconut rice / wild rice
- Top with: pomegranate arils

ROAST SPATCHCOCK CHICKEN & WINGS

Serves: 4-6 • Prep Time: 20 minutes • Cook Time: 30-45 minutes

● **PALEO** ● GRAIN-FREE ● **NUTRIENT DENSE**

Here she is: my low effort, big stunner recipe. Roasted chicken in most any form is my comfort food. Something about that crisp skin, warmed through, served up with an array of cozy or crisp sides: and so much bang for your effort. Wings are also an easy button protein during the week that take very little effort and turn out amazing.

EASY WINGS

ingredients

- 2-4 pastured chicken wings per person
- Coconut Oil, melted
- Seasoning of your Choice (I love Herbamare Herbed Sea Salt, lots!)

Helpful Tip:

I LOVE to serve wings with the Hey Hey Ranch for dipping or the mustard and olive oil dressing with a heavy pour of honey mixed in makes a fab dip, too!

instructions:

1. Preheat oven to 425°F.
2. Rinse wings and remove any feathers. If you'd rather, use kitchen shears and separate the drumette from the wingette. I don't mind them together, your preference wins here.
3. Pat dry and prepare a baking sheet with parchment paper.
4. Position wings on baking sheet with 2-3 inches space, to allow for more crisping.
5. Baste wings lightly with coconut oil, sprinkle with seasoning of choice.
6. Add to center racks of the oven, drop temperature to 400°F. Bake 15 mins. Turn wings over, lightly basting with coconut oil and seasoning the opposite side. Bake 15 minutes.
7. Turn wings one last time to their starting side, baste if needed and leave in to desired crispness. Often they're done at this point, often 5-10 minutes more is all they need.

ROAST SPATCHCOCK CHICKEN & WINGS CONT.

1 Pre-Cooked Pound Per Person • Prep Time: 15 minutes • Cook Time: about 10 minutes per pound

● **PALEO** ● GRAIN-FREE ● **NUTRIENT DENSE**

Ideally, this recipe is a 2-step process: marinate first, then prep to bake. I like to marinate 30 minutes to 4 hours, but not much longer, because the citrus in the marinade will begin cooking the chicken, which we don't want.

Before you begin, take your whole chicken and spatchcock her. This will cut down on cooking time tremendously and leave you some great bones for making broth later.

1. You'll want your sharp cooking shears and a freezer ziplock handy. I like to do this on a sanitizable cutting board next to the sink.
2. Many whole chickens come with the neck and organs tucked neatly inside. You'll remove these and any plastic associated; all chicken parts into the freezer bag for broth making and any plastic to the trash.
3. Cut along the right of the backbone, from the tail to the neck. Cut along the left side to remove the backbone. Toss the backbone into your freezer bag.
4. Flatten down the bird, onto the wings, by breaking the breastbone as your press the chicken flat. You may choose to snip the wing tips at this point and add to your broth bag, or you may tuck them under the bird during cooking time - your call!
5. Add to a casserole dish that fits the chicken snugly or put into a plastic bag to marinate.

CITRUS GARLIC MARINADE

ingredients

- 1 tablespoon fine sea salt
- ½ cup orange juice
- Juice of 1 lemon
- 4 cloves garlic, minced

Marinate up to 4 hours.

PICKLE JUICE MARINADE

ingredients

- 1-2 cups pickle juice, dill or sweet
- 2 teaspoons coarse sea salt
- 1 teaspoon ground black pepper
- Pinch cayenne pepper, if desired
- If dill juice, add: 1 tablespoon coconut sugar

Marinate up to 24 hours.

ROASTED CHICKEN

instructions:

1. Preheat oven to 450°F.
2. Remove marinade from the chicken and add to a casserole dish or roasting pan with sides.
3. Season with salt and pepper. Add ½ tablespoon slices of butter between the skin and flesh of the chicken. This is what makes for magical skin. Dairy free? Bits of coconut oil or duck fat do the trick, too!
4. Tuck citrus slices, herb sprigs of your choosing under the chicken, placing the chicken on top, skin-side up.
5. Move pan to the oven, dropping the temperature to 400°F. After 30 minutes, baste the chicken with juices from the pan, simply squeezing all over the skin. I do this every 5 minutes until a thermometer inserted into the thickest part of the thigh registers 165°F, about 40 minutes for a 4 pound chicken.
6. Let the chicken rest for 5 minutes before serving. Enjoy everyone's awe and amazement that you baked such a beautiful dinner on a weekday.

Pro Tips:

Roasting 2 chickens is the same as roasting 1. I love to serve this on a Sunday, one for the dinner and the other to pick apart and use for chicken salad or tossing in the buffalo chicken casserole later in the week.

Always reserve the bones, tossing them in a freezer bag. When you have a little more time or want those cozy weekend smells, you can cook up nutrient-dense bone broth from the frozen bones.

INSTAPOT CHICKEN BOWL THIGHS

Serves: 4-6 • Prep Time: 5 mins • Cook Time: 12-15 mins

● **PALEO** ● GRAIN-FREE

We love to cook up these delicious chicken thighs for dinner and serve them a few ways throughout the next few days.

ingredients

- 1 tablespoon coconut oil
- 2 pounds boneless chicken thighs, cut into 1" pieces
- Salt and pepper
- 1 cup chicken bone broth
- 2-3 tablespoons balsamic vinegar or apple cider vinegar
- 1 tablespoon garlic powder
- 1 tablespoon onion powder
- Salt
- 4-6 cloves of fresh garlic rough chopped
- ¼ cup thyme (or rosemary or combination of both)

instructions:

1. Turn on Instapot to saute. Add 1 tablespoon coconut oil. Add boneless chicken thighs, cut into 1" pieces and seasoned with salt and pepper. Let them cook until they brown, stir once.
2. While chicken thighs are browning, whisk together the sauce -- chicken bone broth, balsamic vinegar, garlic powder, onion powder, garlic cloves, and salt.
3. Dump sauce over browned chicken. The meat will still have pink, uncooked parts. Stir to combine. Add herbs & cook on medium pressure for 12 min.

TIP: If you don't have an Instapot, add a lid to your skillet and allow to cook on medium-low until all pieces are cooked through and very tender.

INSTAPOT PULLED PORK BUTT

Serves: 8-12 • Prep Time: 10 mins • Cook Time: 75 mins

● **PALEO** ● GRAIN-FREE

This is my go-to pressure cooker pork marinade. Pulled pork is a family workhorse because flavorful meat can anchor a multitude of buddha bowls, tacos and more. You can easily cook a large quantity up and sometimes I'll even toss half the finished product in the freezer for an easy Friday afternoon thaw out.

ingredients

- 3-4 Pound Pork butt or shoulder

For the marinade:

- ⅓ cup coconut aminos
- ¼ cup worcestershire
- 2-4 cloves minced garlic
- 2 tablespoons Italian seasoning
- 2 lemons juice
- ¼ cup avocado oil

instructions:

1. Chop pork butt into 3-4 large chunks. This will allow for more even cooking.
2. Season meat with salt and pepper.
3. Turn on Instapot to saute, add 1-2 tablespoons lard, bacon fat or tallow.
4. Add pork, searing all sides until some browning and caramelization occur.
5. Mix together marinade in a mason jar or bowl and shake or whisk to combine.
6. Once all sides are seared, arrange in a single layer on the bottom of the pot. Pour marinade over pork. Close lid, turn steam valve to "sealing" and set on high pressure for 65 minutes.
7. Once the timer goes off, turn the steam valve to "release" and allow steam to release naturally.
8. Remove lid and allow to cook for 5-10 minutes. Shred meat with forks and serve.

RANCH ROAST

Serves: 4-6 • Prep Time: 15 minutes • Cook Time: 20-90 minutes

● **PALEO**   ● GRAIN-FREE

ingredients

- 1 beef or venison roast (rib roast, round tip roast, rump roast)
- 2 tablespoons dill
- 2 teaspoons garlic powder
- ½ teaspoons onion powder
- Salt and pepper
- 5-8 whole carrots
- 2 cups of root veggies
- ½ cabbage quartered

instructions:

1. Rub the roast down with salt and pepper, seasoning mix.
2. Add to crock pot with a bit of beef stock, chicken stock or water.
3. Cook to half done and add carrots cut to 4-5 inch pieces, quarter sections of potato, sweet potato, parsnip, rutabaga, turnip or a mix of all.

TIP: Total cooking time will depend on the size of your roast. When using the slow cooker, I like to allow 1 ½ hours per pound of roast. In the Instapot, roasts require 20-22 minutes on high pressure to cook to very tender.

GARLIC SESAME CHICKEN

Serves: 4 • Prep Time: 5 minutes • Cook Time: 20 minutes

● **PALEO** ● **GRAIN-FREE**

ingredients

- 4 Boneless, skinless chicken breast sliced thinly lengthwise
- Avocado oil
- ¼ cup sesame seeds
- 1 clove garlic, minced
- ½ cup fresh parsley
- Sea salt and pepper

instructions:

1. Preheat oven to 400°F.
2. Place ingredients other than chicken in bag and shake to mix.
3. Lighty brush chicken with avocado oil. Place one piece of chicken at a time in bag and coat.
4. Place on liberally oiled baking sheet or stone.
5. Bake approximately 20 minutes, turning halfway through.

   TIP: This is one of my most favorite proteins to toss on top of most any of the slaws or the greek salad. Yum and texture-town.

GARLIC SALMON FILETS

Serves: 4 • Prep Time: 15 mins • Cook Time: 12

● PALEO ● GUT HEALTH ● NUTRIENT DENSE

ingredients

- 4 Wild Caught Salmon filets, skin removed
- ⅓ cup extra virgin olive oil, avocado or fractionated coconut oil
- 2 garlic cloves per filet, minced or pressed
- 1 complimentary herb of your choice - I like dill (ranch dressing and lemon a great compliment) or oregano for mediterranean flavor or a ginger for asian flavor

instructions:

Combine olive oil and garlic. Marinade salmon fillets for 5 to 10 minutes. Broil, bake or sauté to desired doneness.

MAPLE MUSTARD SALMON

Serves: 4 • Prep Time: 15 mins • Cook Time: 12 mins

● GRAIN-FREE ● GUT HEALTH ● NUTRIENT DENSE

ingredients

- 4 Wild Caught Salmon filets, skin removed
- ¼ cup mustard
- ¼ cup maple syrup
- 2 tablespoons flax seed
- Sea Salt

instructions:

1. Preheat oven to 350°F.
2. Combine mustard, maple syrup and flax seed - allow to sit 2-3 minutes until thickened.
3. Place a sheet or parchment paper on a baking sheet, add salmon.
4. Season salmon with salt, spoon mixture on top.
5. Bake for 10-14 minutes, until flesh is firm or desired level of doneness.

MEDITERRANEAN TAPENADE SALMON

Serves: 4 • Prep Time: 15 minutes • Cook Time: 12 minutes

● PALEO ● GRAIN-FREE ● GUT HEALTH ● **NUTRIENT DENSE**

ingredients

- 1 cup tomatoes, chopped (I like cherries or heirloom tomatoes)
- 3 tablespoons olive oil
- 1 tablespoon red wine vinegar
- ½ cup kalamata olives, pitted and chopped
- ¼ cup red onion, chopped
- 2 tablespoons capers, drained
- Sea salt and pepper
- 1 tablespoon coconut or avocado oil
- 4 (4-6 ounce) Wild Caught Salmon Filets
- ½ cup fresh basil, chopped

instructions:

1. In a medium bowl, combine tomatoes, olive oil, vinegar, onion, capers, salt and pepper. Set aside.
2. In a saucepan, heat coconut oil at medium-high heat. Sauté salmon 3-4 minutes per side or until cooked through.
3. Add basil to the reserved tomato mixture and serve with salmon.

PORK CHOP N' APPLES

Serves: 4 • Prep Time: 15 minutes • Cook Time: 20 minutes

● PALEO ● GRAIN-FREE

ingredients

- 4 Pastured porkchops
- 4 apples (granny smith or 1-2 varieties for texture variation)
- 2 large sweet onions
- sage or rosemary
- salt and pepper to taste

instructions:

1. Preheat oven to 375°F.
2. Heat cast iron skillet over medium heat.
3. Place porkchops on a plate, lined with paper towel to absorb any excess moisture. Season both sides of the porkchop liberally with salt, pepper and sage or rosemary.
4. Core and slice apples, leaving skins on. I prefer a variety of slice widths so some wither and others are firm. Slice onions in strips.
5. Add a bit of bacon fat, lard or even coconut oil to the pan. Add onions, cook 3-5 minutes until withering.
6. Add apples to the skillet with onions. Cook until some apples begin to be translucent. Remove to a plate.
7. Return pan to medium high heat. A droplet or two of water should quickly sizzle. If porkchops have fatty caps or ends, using tongs, apply the fatty portion to the pan, allowing some fat to render and chop to get crisp on that side. Once some fat is rendered, place chops full side down. Cook until easily removable from the pan, a browning crisp coat should have formed. Flip to other side until the same happens.
8. Return onions and apples to the pan, around the porkchops, not on top of as much as possible. Place whole pan into oven, cooking until porkchop center reaches 140-145°F. Remove from heat. Allow to rest in pan 5 minutes before serving. Remember that meat will continue to cook after removal from the heat.

SWEET GREEN SHEET PAN DINNER

Serves: 4 • Prep Time: 10 minutes • Cook Time: 30 minutes

● **PALEO** ● **GRAIN-FREE**

ingredients

- 2 medium sweet potatoes
- 3 cups brussel sprouts
- 1 package andouille sausage
- 3 tablespoons avocado oil
- 1 teaspoon ceylon cinnamon
- 2 teaspoons coarse sea salt
- 1 teaspoon ground black pepper

instructions:

1. Preheat oven to 400°F.
2. Cut sweet potatoes into cubes and coat with 1 tablespoon avocado oil. Sprinkle with salt, pepper, and cinnamon.
3. Place in oven for 15 minutes.
4. While sweet potatoes are baking, cut the ends off the brussel sprouts and cut in half. Next, cut the sausage into even ½ inch slices. Toss the brussels and sausage in the remaining oil, and season with salt and pepper.
5. When the timer goes off, add the brussels and sausage to the sheet pan mixing in with the sweet potatoes, add a pinch more salt and pepper, and return to the oven for an additional 15 minutes.
6. Allow to cool slightly, and enjoy!

TIP: Don't forget to add a sheet of parchment paper to your pan before you add your food and cleanup will be a snap. Most folks have aluminum sheet pans, this steps allows another layer of protection against the aluminum.

HARVEST SHEET PAN DINNER

Serves: 4 • Prep Time: 10 minutes • Cook Time: 30 minutes

● **PALEO** ● GRAIN-FREE

ingredients

- 1 large green or red apple, tart!
- 3 cups acorn squash, cut into cubes (about 1 squash)
- 1 yellow onion
- 1 cup cranberries, frozen or fresh
- 4 pasture raised chicken sausages, precooked
- 3 tablespoons avocado oil
- Juice from ½ an orange
- 1 teaspoon coarse sea salt
- 1 teaspoon fresh black pepper
- 1 teaspoon dried thyme leaves

instructions:

1. Preheat oven to 400°F.
2. Cube the apple, to match the size of the cubed squash. Cut the onion into wedges and spread apple, squash, onion and cranberries onto a lined sheet pan.
3. Drizzle avocado oil over the items on sheet pan and then season with salt, pepper, and dried thyme leaves.
4. Place pan in oven to bake for 15 minutes. Meanwhile, cut the sausages into inch thick slices.
5. Remove pan from oven, add the sliced sausage onto the pan, squeeze the orange over the sheet pan allowing the juice to lightly coat items and then place pan back in the oven for an additional 15 minutes.
6. Let cool slightly, and then serve!

TIP: Don't forget to add a sheet of parchment paper to your pan before you add your food and cleanup will be a snap.

TIP: I also love to add a bundle of brussel sprouts to the mix for a greens boost.

QUICK CHICKEN STIR-FRY

Serves: 4 • Prep Time: 10 minutes • Cook Time: 15 minutes

● GRAIN-FREE

ingredients

- 2 boneless, skinless chicken breast, sliced into strips
- 1 tablespoon grated fresh ginger
- 3 garlic cloves, minced
- 3 teaspoons coconut or sesame oil to coat the pan
- 1 medium onion, sliced or diced
- 2-3 cups any combination of chopped veggies – bok choy, celery, carrots, broccoli florets, Napa cabbage, snap peas, snow peas, baby corn, etc.
- 1 can sliced water chestnuts or bamboo shoots, drained
- 1 cup sliced mushrooms – preferably shiitake
- 1 red bell pepper, cut into strips
- If not using mushrooms or bell pepper, replace with more of another vegetable
- ¼ cup coconut aminos
- Juice 1 orange or ¼ cup orange juice
- 1 tablespoon honey
- Sesame seeds and or furikake for seasoning

instructions:

1. Heat oil in wok or large skillet over high heat. Once heated, add garlic, ginger and chicken stir constantly until lightly brown or chicken cooked through.
2. Add all vegetables and cook for 3-4 minutes to maintain crispness.
3. Mix coconut aminos, honey and orange juice in a bowl.
4. Pour sauce mixture and sesame seeds over stir fry until coated, remove from heat.

TIP: This recipe is the most flexible and can easily bring together the week's leftover veggies into one cohesive meal.

ROAST LEMON CHICKEN PICCATA

Serves: 4 • Prep Time: 10 minutes • Cook Time: 15 minutes

● **PALEO** ● **GRAIN-FREE**

ingredients

- 4 chicken breasts
- ½ teaspoon dried thyme
- ¼ teaspoon salt
- ¼ teaspoon pepper
- 2 garlic cloves, pressed
- 1 cup cherry tomatoes
- ½ cup chicken stock
- ½ teaspoon lemon peel
- 2 tablespoons lemon juice
- 1 tablespoon olive or coconut oil
- Optional: 3 tablespoons capers

Helpful Tip:

We love this with quick, steamed broccoli. Simple and fresh. Bonus points for extra lemon juice over the broccoli!

instructions:

1. Preheat oven to 400°F.
2. Lightly oil broiler pan with a small amount of olive oil.
3. Pound chicken out until thin and even. I toss chicken in a ziplock or between 2 layers of plastic wrap and pound with the bottom of a saucepan. Season both sides of chicken with thyme, pepper, and ⅛ teaspoon salt.
4. Cook in oven on center rack for 10 minutes.
5. Change heat to broiler.
6. Place pan about 3-5 inches from the heat for 3-5 minutes per side or until 160°F at thickest part. Remove from broiler and keep warm.
7. Heat a large skillet with a bit of bacon grease or avocado oil over medium heat. Add garlic and stir constantly for 30 seconds. Add tomatoes and remaining ⅛ teaspoon salt and cook for 3 minutes. Place tomatoes on platter with chicken.
8. In the same skillet, whisk together chicken broth, lemon peel and lemon juice and bring to a boil over high heat while stirring constantly. Cook for one minute.
9. Add oil and any juice collected on platter and simmer while stirring constantly. Cook until sauce thickens slightly. Add capers, if using. Pour over the chicken and serve.

CHICKEN CACCIATORE

Serves: 4 • Prep Time: 15 minutes • Cook Time: 20 minutes

● **PALEO** ● **GRAIN-FREE**

ingredients

- ½ cup plus 2 tablespoons extra virgin olive oil
- 2 garlic cloves, pressed
- 2 tablespoons balsamic vinegar
- 1 tablespoon gluten free worcestershire
- 1 teaspoon crushed red pepper flakes
- 1 package button mushrooms, sliced
- 3 teaspoons fresh rosemary, 5 sprigs stripped and leaves chopped
- 4 boneless, skinless breasts
- Sea salt and pepper
- 1 medium red onion, thinly sliced
- 1 28-ounce can fire-roasted diced or crushed tomatoes (lightly drained)
- Handful of flat-leaf (Italian) parsley, chopped

Helpful Tip:

You do not want to use a cast iron skillet as the acid involved in the recipe will corrode the pan's seasoned surface.

instructions:

1. Heat a grill pan or outdoor grill to high heat. You can also use a large heavy bottomed pan on the stove for cooking the chicken.
2. In a large bowl, combine balsamic vinegar, worcestershire, crushed red pepper flakes and rosemary. Whisk in about ½ cup extra virgin olive oil. Briefly marinate the mushrooms in this mixture. Remove and set aside.
3. Add chicken to remaining marinade and coat evenly.
4. Let sit for 2-3 minutes.
5. Add chicken to hot pan or grill, cooking until chicken easily releases. Season the visible side of the chicken with salt and pepper while cooking. Turn. Cook chicken until registering 165°F at the thickest point. Remove to serving platter.
6. Season mushrooms with pepper only. Add 1 tablespoon olive oil into a hot skillet. Cook mushrooms only until they begin releasing water - remember, no salt is key. Add garlic, onions to skillet. Cook and toss frequently for approximately 7-8 minutes.
7. Add tomatoes and parsley, salt and pepper and heat through, approximately 1 minute. Remove from heat.
8. Thinly slice chicken and arrange on platter or serve whole. Cover with the sauce mixture and serve.

VEGGIE ANGEL HAIR PASTA

Prep Time: 10 minutes • Cook Time: 30 minutes

● **PALEO** ● GRAIN-FREE

ingredients

- 3 zucchinis
- 16 ounce cherry tomatoes (candy like) or 1 pound roma type tomatoes
- ½ sweet onion
- 4 fresh basil leaves
- 1 **or** 2 cloves garlic
- 1 red, orange **or** yellow bell pepper (not green)
- 1 tablespoon dried Italian spices **or** oregano, basil, salt & pepper
- Olive oil

instructions:

1. Use a spiralizer to cut zucchini into angel hair like strands. This can be prepared days in advance, stored in the fridge (water will evaporate and the noodle becomes more stiff). Place all remaining items in a food processor or blender and pulse to chop to a "chunky" consistency. Do not puree down to thinner than a large pico texture. Pour sauce into a pan on medium low (no lid) and allow to come together for 30 minutes to allow sauce to evaporate and thicken. Pour over zucchini pasta. Do not cook zucchini pasta - allow sauce to warm it.

BUFFALO CHICKEN CASSEROLE

Serves: 10 • Prep Time: 15 minutes • Cook Time: 45 minutes
● **PALEO** ● GRAIN-FREE

I like to serve this over chopped romaine lettuce or crispy, shredded napa cabbage. Is great with coconut rice as well as served for a dip in a party occasion served with grain-free tortilla chips or plantain chips. To prepare as a dip, chop everything very fine.

ingredients

- 2 pounds cooked chicken, shredded
- 16 ounces cauliflower rice, frozen
- 1 sweet white onion, diced
- 1 red pepper, diced
- 1-2 jalapenos, finely diced; more for topping if desired
- 1 cup shredded carrots
- ½ cup coconut cream, canned
- ½ cup prepared buffalo sauce
- ¼ cup Hey Hey Ranch
- 2 tablespoons minced garlic
- 1 teaspoon salt
- ½ teaspoon black pepper
- Garnishes: jalapenos, chopped scallions

instructions:

1. Preheat oven to 400°F.
2. Dump shredded chicken and vegetables into a large bowl. Stir and be sure all vegetables are evenly distributed.
3. Combine remaining spices, buffalo sauce, ranch, coconut cream, minced garlic, salt and pepper. Whisk to combine. Can also be tossed in the blender to be sure the coconut cream fully distributes.
4. Pour into the bowl to evenly distributed over chicken mixture. Combine best as possible. Pour into a 9 by 13 inch casserole dish, smoothing the ingredients into a solid layer.
5. Bake in the oven for 45 minutes. If you prefer a more crisp crusty top, switch to the broiler for 2-5 minutes at the end.
6. Remove from oven. Garnish slices with jalapeno peppers, chopped scallions, additional buffalo sauce.

hey hey
SOUPS

INTRO INTO PHO SOUPS
stocks & broths

● PALEO ● GRAIN-FREE ● GUT HEALTH ● NUTRIENT DENSE

Is it food? Is it medicine? Broths are both! If broth is the single thing you take from this cookbook and implement into your life, health will increase.

Broths have been a healing tool for ages because of the pre-digested nutrient-density. When bones are slow cooked alongside vegetables, the minerals and amino acids leave the bones, making for a rich, gelatinous broth. While it used to gross me out, broth that jiggles once cooled is the magic spot. Bones have released their gelatin and collagen - two big tools - along with amino acids arginine and glycine, for gut healing. Broth is also my go-to protein for boosting children who don't yet love proteins. I tell every friend with an infant to introduce bone broth alongside solids, adding a drop of sauerkraut juice to the cup. The kiddos I know started this way, have such robust health and are open to a variety of foods.

BONE BROTH

- 4 pounds cooked chicken, beef or bison bones
- 1-2 chicken feet (optional)
- 2 tablespoons apple cider vinegar
- 1 head garlic, cut in half, through the cloves
- 1 onion, roughly quartered, skin on
- 2 carrots, roughly chopped
- 2 celery stalks, roughly chopped
- 1 tablespoon whole peppercorns
- 1 bay leaf

CHICKEN BONE BROTH

- 2 chicken caracasses
- 1-2 chicken feet or several wing bones (optional)
- 2 tablespoons apple cider vinegar
- 1 head garlic, cut in half, through the cloves
- 1 large onion, quartered, skin on
- 2 carrots, roughly chopped
- 2 celery stalks, roughly chopped
- 1 tablespoons whole peppercorns
- 1 bay leaf

CHICKEN STOCK

- 4 pounds cooked chicken, beef or 1 whole 3-4 pound chicken
- 1-2 chicken feet or several wing bones (optional)
- 2 tablespoons apple cider vinegar
- 1 head garlic, cut in half, through the cloves
- 1 large onion, quartered, skin on
- 2 carrots, roughly chopped
- 2 celery stalks, roughly chopped
- 1 tablespoon whole peppercorns
- 1 bay leaf

INSTAPOT PROCESS

- Add all materials to the Instapot.
- Cover, to fill line with filtered water.
- For bone broths, set at high pressure for 2 hours with a natural release. For chicken stock, cook for 45 minutes at high pressure with a natural release; remove carcass and reserve meat. Bones can be used again for bone broth if only used for chicken stock.
- Strain broth through a fine mesh strainer and store.

SLOW COOKER PROCESS

- Add all materials to the slow cooker.
- Cover completely with filtered water.
- For bone broths, set to low, simmering for 24 hours. Skim and discard any foam that rises to the surface during cooking. For chicken stock, cook for 4 hours on high or 8 hours on low; remove carcass and reserve meat. Bones can be used again for bone broth if only used for chicken stock.
- Strain broth through a fine mesh strainer and store.

storage options

Save it up: Keep a freezer bag or two in the freezer for catching leftover bones, onion, celery and carrot scraps. Stockpile in the bag until full, then you're ready to make a batch.

Season: I love to add herbs to stocks and broths, but remember, the more neutral you make the flavor, the more you can bend it later. For example, I simmer star anise and a cinnamon stick when heating pho broth or some fresh sage when I use stock for a sausage soup. The same goes for salt, you can't take it out once added, so I reserve all salt seasoning until I'm making the final meal.

Vary storage: Tossing stock into the freezer is the perfect way to save it. I'll keep old yogurt containers, to-go containers, various mason jars and utilize silicone baking or ice cube trays. You want stock that's easy to thaw for a quick cup, a couple tablespoons in a dish, 2 cups for cooking rice in or larger servings for making soups and stews. Be sure to leave head room in any container you use - broth, like water, expands a bit when frozen.

Save the fat: Once the broth has cooled and any fat has risen to the top, scrape it off and store in a refrigerated mason jar, using in recipes as you would other animal fats.

LIMITLESS CHICKEN SOUP

Serves: 8 • Prep Time: 10 minutes • Cook Time: 30 minutes

● **PALEO** ● GRAIN-FREE ● **GUT HEALTH** ● **NUTRIENT DENSE**

The magic of this soup happens when you make it with a rotisserie chicken from the store. It comes together quickly, the chicken falls apart and nearly forms a cozy stew at the reheat. We love to serve it over chopped kale, cooked wild rice or a quick cooked rice ramen. I've been known to throw rice pho noodles straight in the pot when serving it to a crowd immediately.

ingredients

- 2 tablespoons healthy fat
- 1 sweet onion, diced
- 2 garlic cloves, minced
- 5 large carrots, chopped
- 5 stalks celery, chopped
- 8-12 cups chicken stock
- 1 bay leaf
- 2 tablespoons dried thyme
- 4 cups cooked shredded chicken
- Salt and pepper to taste

instructions:

1. Heat fat in a stock pot or dutch oven over medium heat. Once melted, add onions and cook until golden. Season with salt.
2. Add garlic, stirring until fragrant.
3. Add carrots and celery, cooking 5-6 minutes. Season with salt and pepper.
4. Add chicken stock, bay leaf and thyme. Add chicken and simmer a bit.

TIP: Add a can of coconut cream, one can of green chilis and a can of white northern beans and you've got yourself a white chicken chili. When I do this, I toss in a couple teaspoons of paprika and a dash of cayenne pepper.

PENNY'S VEGETABLE SOUP

Serves: 8-12 • Prep Time: 20 minutes • Cook Time: 90 minutes

● PALEO ● GRAIN-FREE ● GUT HEALTH ● NUTRIENT DENSE

This is our family go-to soup. You know the one - you pull it out the moment it feels like a fall day has arrived on a weekend. You can also take the option to uplevel the nutrient content to be a beef vegetable soup - just add some 100% Grass-fed beef stew meat. I love to work this in, as it's a lesser cut of meat, which means lesser cost and when it's cooked down in a soup, the texture comes around to tender just fine.

ingredients

- 2 tablespoons butter or coconut oil or bacon fat or lard
- 2 cups chopped onions or leeks (or combination of both)
- 1 tablespoon minced garlic
- 1 can organic fire roasted san marzano tomatoes (up to you the size can, or can be omitted for nightshade free)
- 1 cup thinly sliced carrots
- 1 cup finely sliced celery

- 4 cups chicken broth
- 4 cups beef broth
- 2 cans organic green beans
- 1 cup sliced turnips or sweet potato or potato
- 1 can organic sweet corn
- 1 can organic peas
- 1 ½ cups thinly sliced cabbage or kale
- 1-2 tablespoons herbs fresh or dried (basil, oregano, italian seasoning, parsley)

instructions:

1. In a stock pot, melt butter. Add onions or leeks and cook until browning begins.
2. Add celery and carrots, cooking for a few minutes to soften, add garlic just before adding tomatoes.
3. Add tomatoes, broth, seasoning with salt and pepper.
4. Add green beans, turnip or potato or sweet potato, sweet corn and peas.
5. Simmer for 20-30 mins.
6. Add cabbage and herbs at the end.

This recipe is very forgiving and flexible. The mix of herbs can be shifted and we often serve this over some chickpea noodles, wild rice or rotisserie chicken.

TIP: If using beef, your first step will be to brown the meat in a bit of oil, cut into 1 inch pieces. Remove the meat, add the onions or leeks. Cook until all is browned, adding garlic at the end. Add beef, stocks and simmer on low for 1 hour. Once beef is fork tender, you may add remaining ingredients.

KALE, SAUSAGE, POTATO

Serves: 8-12 • Prep Time: 15 minutes • Cook Time: 90 minutes

● PALEO ● GRAIN-FREE ● GUT HEALTH ● **NUTRIENT DENSE**

ingredients

- 1 pound ground pork - sage, plain or italian seasoned
- 1-2 tablespoons dried sage
- 2 small yellow onions, diced
- 3 cartons or 12 cups bone/chicken broths - can use a mix of chicken/beef
- 2 cups sweet potato, diced
- 1-2 tablespoons salt to taste
- 1 bay leaf
- 12 ounce bag curly kale, destemmed and chopped

instructions:

1. In a large soup pan or dutch oven, brown pork on low, adding sage as it cooks - cook until most pink is gone. Remove to bowl.
2. Add onions to the remaining pork fat. Cook on medium-low, 10-20 mins until onions have browned.
3. Add bay leaves, stock, salt and stir. Bring to a gentle simmer. Add in potatoes and cooked sausage. Simmer until potatoes are fork tender. Add bag of kale, removing from heat.

SERVING TIP: When you're ready to serve, I like to add a tablespoon of coconut cream in the bottom of the bowl. You can quick fry some sage leaves in coconut oil and Maldon sea salt too!

LEMON CHICKEN TURMERIC GINGER SOUP

Serves: 8 • Prep Time: 5 minutes • Cook Time: 30 minutes

● PALEO ● GRAIN-FREE ● GUT HEALTH ● **NUTRIENT DENSE**

Kick back a cold or enjoy a cozy cup of this comforting Lemon Chicken Turmeric Ginger. Paleo, dairy-free, gluten-free, Whole 30 & anti-inflammatory. It's my go-to gift for a sick friend.

ingredients

- 1 tablespoon coconut oil
- 1 diced onion
- 3-4 stalks chopped celery
- 3-4 chopped carrots
- 1 teaspoon salt
- 1 tablespoon minced turmeric
- 1-2 tablespoons grated ginger
- 1-3 cloves minced garlic
- ½ teaspoon pepper

- 8 cups bone broth or chicken stock
- 2 cups cooked chicken
- 1-2 diced zuchinnis
- 1-2 cups coconut milk
- juice of 1 lemon
- 1-2 tablespoons parsley
- optional garnish cilantro

instructions:

1. Melt coconut oil in your favorite stock or pan.
2. Add celery, carrots and onion. Cook until soft.
3. Add salt, pepper, turmeric, garlic, & ginger. Combine to coat veggies.
4. Add bone broth or chicken stock and bring to a simmer. Simmer 5 mins.
5. Add zucchini and salt and pepper to taste. Simmer 5 minutes.
6. Add coconut milk, lemon juice and parsley. Stir to combine.

TIP: Garnished with a bit of cilantro, if you wish, this soup really shines.

ROASTED SWEET POTATO SOUP

Serves: 4 • Prep Time: 30 minutes • Cook Time: 20 minutes

● PALEO ● GRAIN-FREE ● **GUT HEALTH** ● **NUTRIENT DENSE**

ingredients

- 5 medium sweet potatoes, peeled and sliced
- 1 head of garlic
- 1 medium sweet onion, chopped
- ½ red onion, chopped
- 2 tablespoons olive oil, divided
- 6 cups chicken broth

instructions:

1. Preheat oven to 350°F.
2. Rub potatoes with 1 tablespoon of the olive oil and place on baking sheet.
3. Wrap the head of garlic in aluminum foil and place on baking sheet with potatoes. Bake for 30 minutes or until potatoes are soft.
4. Heat remaining oil in a medium sauté pan with the onion until it is translucent, about 3 minutes.
5. In a blender or food processor, add onion, garlic, and near half of the potatoes. Puree thoroughly. Transfer to a large pot and add all remaining ingredients. Heat to a boil, then lower heat and allow to simmer for about 15 minutes. You can also add all ingredients to the pot, immersion blend to combine, in the pot.

TIP: I love to serve this with a spoon of coconut cream, roasted pumpkin seeds, pomegranate arils and fried sage leaves.

hey hey
SNACKS

ELDERBERRY SYRUP GUMMIES

Serves: 2 cups of gummies • Prep Time: 3 minutes • Cook Time: 10 minutes

● PALEO ● GRAIN-FREE ● **GUT HEALTH** ● **NUTRIENT DENSE**

I often serve 1-2 gummies as dessert to lunch on our school days or for a snack here and there. I've also subbed the pomegranate for other juices that I had on hand and they've worked great. I love to choose raw, local honey when possible, too - but often squeeze in my Costco honey. For a fun little sour boost, I'll roll them in Natural Calm Magnesium powder right before serving or dip the Lego mold gummies' feet in the powder and call them snow day lego guys. Possibilities are endless! Enjoy!

ingredients

- ¼ cup Elderberry Syrup
- 1 cup juice (antioxidant blends are my fave; apple and pomegranate combined are also great!)
- 2 tablespoons lemon juice
- 2 tablespoons honey
- ¼ cup gelatin

instructions:

1. Combine all ingredients in a pan over medium heat, except gelatin. Bring just to before simmer.
2. Whisk in gelatin. Pour slowly to avoid clumping and whisk until combined.
3. Reduce heat and leave at just below a simmer 8-10 minutes, whisking occasionally.
4. Remove from heat and promptly divide among silicone trays using a turkey baster. Place in fridge to set.

LOVE YOUR LIVER DANDELION MOCHA

Serves: 1 • Prep Time: 3 minutes • Cook Time: 10 minutes

● **PALEO** ● **GRAIN-FREE** ● **GUT HEALTH** ● **NUTRIENT DENSE**

ingredients

- 1 cup brewed dandelion tea
- 1 tablespoon coconut butter or oil
- 1 teaspoon cinnamon
- 1 tablespoon cocoa powder
- ¼ cup coconut cream or milk of choice

instructions:

Mix all ingredients together & enjoy! If you have a frother, this makes it extra yummy!

Kick candida, love your liver, enjoy a yummy little treat while you detox.

FALL MIX

Serves: 12 • Prep Time: 15 minutes • Cook Time: 1 hour

ingredients

- 9 cups rice squares cereal (like Rice Chex™ or Rice Bitz)
- 1 cup mixed nuts (we like to use a mix of raw and unroasted)
- 1 cup gluten free pretzels (I love Snyders of Hanover pretzel sticks)
- 1 cup plantain chips

- 6 tablespoons coconut oil
- 2 tablespoons Worcestershire sauce **or** coconut aminos (make sure it's gluten free!)
- 3 teaspoons seasoned salt
- ¾ teaspoon garlic powder
- ½ teaspoon onion powder

instructions:

1. Pre-heat oven to 250°F.
2. Gently mix together cereal, nuts, pretzels and plantain chips. Spread on a few cookie sheets.
3. Stir together coconut oil (you may need to warm this up to melt), worcestershire sauce, salt, garlic powder and onion powder. Pour over cereal mixture on cookie sheets.
4. Bake for 1 hour, stirring every 15 minutes.

Once baked, spread out onto paper towels until cool. Enjoy.

EASY ORANGE (OR ANY) JUICE GUMMIES

Serves: 4 cups of gummies • Prep Time: 3 minutes • Cook Time: 10 minutes

● PALEO ● GRAIN-FREE ● GUT HEALTH ● **NUTRIENT DENSE**

ingredients

- 1 - 32 ounce bottle orange juice
- ¼ cup + 2 tablespoons high quality gelatin

instructions:

1. Heat juice until almost boiling.
2. Sprinkle in the gelatin and stir until dissolved.
3. Slowly pour mixture into silicone molds. You can let this sit on the counter a few minutes until it gels a bit so you don't spill everywhere on your way to the fridge.
4. Transfer to the fridge to completely set (at least 2 hours).

Keep leftovers in refrigerator.

INFAMOUS ADRENAL COCKTAIL

Serves: 1 • Prep Time: 2 minutes

● **PALEO**   ● **GRAIN-FREE**   ● **GUT HEALTH**   ● **NUTRIENT DENSE**

This afternoon pick-me-up is no original - it's sweeped the interwebs - it's also helped sweep my tired, cobwebbed, afternoon Mom-brain on many days. This drink is a game-changing staple! The adrenal cocktail provides a balanced ratio of carbs, protein, and fat that is also loaded with minerals and Vitamin C, which help to regulate blood sugar and give the adrenals a much needed break. When you're dragging, whip one up.

ingredients

- 4 ounces fresh squeezed organic orange juice
- 2 tablespoons coconut cream
- 2 tablespoons collagen
- A hefty pinch of himalayan sea salt (as much as you can tolerate)

instructions:

Shake it in a mason jar or blend it up in your blender.

WATER KEFIR

Serves: Many • Prep Time: 5 active minutes, 24 hours to ferment

● GRAIN-FREE ● **GUT HEALTH**

My hopes for water kefir are high! I keep hoping it'll soon have the moment that sourdough had in 2020. While kefir is traditionally a cultured dairy product, making kefir with water and a bit of sugar is the easiest way to keep a steady flow of probiotic bacteria to your household. I use in a lot of places you'd use water like salad dressing, a splash in a smoothie, even a splash here or there into my kid's breakfast drinks. Water kefir is relatively benign, taste wise, so it's an easy sneak. If you add 2 parts kefir to 1 part juice, the second fermentation will yield a much much gentler drink similar to kombucha - a little efervescent, a light juice flavor.

ingredients

- Kefir Grains (found online or at local small grocers)
- 3 tablespoons organic cane sugar
- Water
- Juice for dilution and second fermentation

instructions:

1. Add grains to jug when just starting or drain the jar down to just grains.
2. Add 3 tablespoons of organic sugar. Organic is imperative in this application, since we're looking to multiply the naturally occurring bacteria in the kefir.
3. Fill jug with room temperature filtered water and cover. Let sit on counter for 24 hours.
4. After 24 hours drain water out into a pitcher for the fridge. Dilute with juice to a ratio of 1 part juice to 2 parts water kefir.
5. You can feed the grains over and over again and use again. If you cannot keep up with your water kefir's production, it is ok to allow it to continue to ferment on the counter. This will make a kefir very similar to vinegar. You can use it as such, or drain and discard, then begin again. If there is every any mold growth you would want to disard all kefir, sanitize the container and begin again. Pictured here, is my Kefirko, the easiest container I have found.

KALE GUACAMOLE

Serves: 2-4 • Prep Time: 15 minutes

● **PALEO** ● **GRAIN-FREE**

ingredients

- 2 cups kale leaves, chopped
- ½ cup fresh cilantro, chopped
- 4 avocados
- ½-1 teaspoon sea salt
- 3 tomatoes, seeded and chopped
- ¼ cup red onion, minced
- 2 jalapenos, seeded and finely chopped (optional)
- Juice of 2 limes

instructions:

1. Place the kale leaves in a food processor and pulse until they are finely chopped. Add cilantro leaves, quickly pulse.
2. Place the avocado flesh in a large bowl, add the salt, and mash until desired texture is reached.
3. Stir in the kale leaves and remaining ingredients. Taste and adjust salt as needed.
4. Serve immediately.

TIP: I love to use this as a spread for lettuce rolls ups. Schmear a bit on the leaf, add leftover protein and whichever veggies you have handy and you've got yourself a quick and easy lunch with a healthy fat!

CILANTRO GUAC – HEAVY METAL HELPER

Serves: 1-3 • Prep Time: 5 minutes

● PALEO ● GRAIN-FREE ● **NUTRIENT DENSE**

ingredients

- ½ cup olive or avocado oil
- 1 bunch fresh cilantro, leaves and stems from bottom leaf up
- 2 avocados
- ½-1 teaspoon sea salt
- 1 clove garlic
- Juice of 1 lime
- Water to consistency

instructions:

1. Place the oil and cilantro leaves, top stems only in a wide mouth, mason pint jar. Using an immersion blender, blend until smooth.
2. Add the avocado flesh, salt, garlic clove and juice of lime to the jar; blend until desired texture is reached.
3. Leave as-is for a guacamole style dip or add water if looking for a looser, more dressing-like consistency. Taste and adjust salt as needed.

Serve immediately. Stores well in fridge with a lid. Top the guac with a thin layer of oil to keep from browning.

heyhey

DESSERTS

DESSERTS

First things first, can we normalize a sweet snack? A snack that's balanced with a protein or fat, but also doesn't get out of control when it comes to portion size? Let's kickoff this chapter with several of my most loved dessert combinations. Sometimes cravings just take a little sweet combo, while other times you just need a full blown dessert or celebration offering for guests. These recipes aren't all sugar free, nor perfect for every diet, but they are a strong pack of favorites, several family faves made over.

- Apple nachos: apple sliced through core, nut butter, coconut, chia seeds, DF chocolate mini-chips
- Applesauce
- Apples + nut butter
- Banana nachos: banana slices, nut butter, coconut, chia
- Banana "nice cream" + almond butter + cocoa
- Bacon wrapped date
- Blueberries + watermelon + mint
- Cinnamon Apples
- Coconut whipped cream with fresh berries
- Coconut cream over frozen berries + chia
- Coconut milk + frozen berries popsicles
- Coconut oil + cocoa powder or chocolate
- Chia pudding: chia + almond milk + add ins: cocoa powder + cayenne OR lemon juice, zest + blueberries + toasted coconut
- Corn tortilla, coconut or almond wrap, nut butter, rolled
- Dates + goat cheese inside
- Dates + nut butter inside + frozen
- Date + butter + salt
- Dehydrated apple chips
- Dried banana chips
- Dried Mango
- Dried Apricots
- Dried apricots + goat or sheep cheese

- Fig wrapped in proscuitto
- Frozen applesauce with a popsicle stick
- Frozen blueberries
- Frozen cherries
- Frozen grapes
- Frozen peach slices
- Frozen fruit, coconut milk poured on top
- Fruit kabobs
- Fruit leather
- Gelatin gummies (coconut whip + bee pollen)
- Gluten free granola
- Grapes dipped in melted coconut butter
- Green smoothie
- Homemade gelatin gummies
- Kettle corn
- Mandarin Orange
- Peach wrapped in proscuitto
- Pineapple + deli ham skewers
- Popsicles made from blended fruit and coconut water or milk
- Protein smoothie
- Watermelon + lime popsicles
- Watermelon + mint (+ honey)
- Watermelon + mint
- Watermelon + sheep's milk feta cheese
- Yogurt (goat/nut based) + honey + chia + frozen fruit
- Yogurt + protein powder bowl w/ mixed nuts or granola

SUNDAY AFTERNOON CHOCOLATE CHEWIES

Serves: 1 dozen cookies • Prep Time: 5 minutes • Cook Time: 10-12 minutes

● GRAIN-FREE

ingredients

- 1 egg
- ½ cup almond butter
- 2 tablespoons coconut sugar or sweetener of choices
- 3-4 tablespoons blanched almond flour
- 1 tablespoons maple syrup
- ½ teaspoon baking soda
- Pinch Salt
- ¼ cup allergen-free chocolate chips (I love Enjoy Life's chips or chunks)

instructions:

1. Preheat oven to 350°F. Line baking sheet with parchment paper.
2. Put all ingredients in one bowl, except chocolate chips.
3. Mix.
4. Fold in chocolate chips.
5. Drop 8 equal sized spoonfuls onto the baking sheet.
6. Bake 10-12 minutes.
7. Press cookies flat a bit, they will not expand while baking.

GUT-LOVING CHOCOLATE CHIP COOKIES

Serves: 1 Dozen Cookies • Prep Time: 10 minutes • Cook Time: 10-12 minutes

● GRAIN-FREE ● **GUT HEALTH**

ingredients

- 1 cup tigernut flour
- ⅔ cup arrowroot powder
- ½ cup coconut oil, softened
- ¼ cup collagen
- ¼ cup honey or maple syrup
- 1 teaspoon vanilla extract
- 1 teaspoon apple cider vinegar
- ½ teaspoon baking soda
- 1 teaspoon cream of tartar
- ¼ teaspoon sea salt
- ⅓ cup allergen-free chocolate chips

Pro Tip:

In this recipe, maple syrup and honey substitute well for one another. If you're on a LOW FODMAP diet, use maple syrup instead of honey. The texture is a bit more chewy with honey, but maple syrup works great, too! I haven't found the rest of the ingredients to be swappable, largely due to the nature of being egg-free and the way both tigernut and arrowroot flours work.

instructions:

1. Preheat oven to 350°F.
2. Line a large baking sheet pan with parchment paper.
3. In a medium bowl, combine all dry ingredients: tigernut flour, arrowroot powder, collagen, baking soda, cream of tartar and sea salt.
4. Melt coconut oil and combine in a separate bowl with wet ingredients: coconut oil, honey or maple syrup, vanilla, apple cider vinegar.
5. Add wet ingredients to dry, mixing by hand or with a mixed until there are no lumps, without over-mixing.
6. Stir in the chocolate chips.
7. Use a cookie dough scoop to portion out dough on a lined cookie sheet.
8. Bake 10-12 minutes until the edges are golden brown and tops are a bit golden. Allow to cool before serving.

COCONUT KEY LIME CHIA PUDDING

Serves: 4-6 • Prep Time: 5 mins • Cook Time: 15 mins

● GRAIN-FREE

ingredients

- 1 can full-fat coconut milk
- 1 tablespoon + 1 teaspoon lime zest
- 1 teaspoon vanilla extract
- ½ cup chia seeds
- 1 tablespoon pure maple syrup (or local honey)
- Juice from 2 limes
- ¼ cup unsweetened shredded coconut (optional)

instructions:

1. In a small pot, bring the canned coconut milk, 1 teaspoon of lime zest, vanilla extract, lime juice, and maple syrup to a low simmer. Whisk until all ingredients are incorporated, letting simmer for 10 minutes.
2. While the coconut milk is simmering, place the chia seeds and the remaining lime zest in a glass mason jar. Add the coconut milk mixture to the jar. Stir to completely mix ingredients, cover, and place in the refrigerator. Shake the jar at least once more about an hour or two later.
3. Store in the refrigerator overnight, and add shredded coconut on top before enjoying!

RASPBERRY LEMON CHIA PUDDING

Serves: 4-6 • Prep Time: 5 mins • Cook Time: 15 mins

● GRAIN-FREE ● **GUT HEALTH**

ingredients

- 1 can full-fat coconut milk
- ½ cup chia seeds
- Zest and juice of ½ lemon
- 1 teaspoon vanilla extract
- 1 cup raspberries (fresh or frozen)
- ½ tablespoon pure maple syrup (or local honey)

instructions:

1. In a small pot, bring coconut milk, lemon juice, lemon zest, vanilla extract and maple syrup to a light boil. Reduce to a simmer and add raspberries. Mash berries with the back of a wooden spoon into the coconut milk mixture. Allow to simmer for 10 minutes. For a smoother texture, you can blend the mixture for a few seconds to fully incorporate the berries.
2. In a glass mason jar, add the chia seeds and then pour the coconut milk mixture. Shake or stir all contents in the jar before placing in the refrigerator. Shake jar once more about an hour or two later and let sit overnight.

ORANGE CREAMSICLE CHIA PUDDING

Serves: 4-6 • Prep Time: 5 mins • Cook Time: 15 mins

● GRAIN-FREE ● **GUT HEALTH**

ingredients

- 2 cups peeled clementine segments plus zest
- 1 can full-fat coconut milk
- ½ cup chia seeds
- 1 teaspoon vanilla extract

instructions:

1. In a small pot, heat the coconut milk, vanilla extract and orange zest to a light boil.
2. Place the heated mixture in a blender with the clementine segments and blend until smooth. Put the chia seeds in a glass mason jar, pouring the coconut milk and orange mixture on top.
3. Shake the jar and place in the refrigerator to chill overnight. Give the jar a good shake an hour or two later, and then continue to chill.

Helpful Tip:

Divide the finished pudding among half pint mason jars for an easy grab and go snack.

SIMPLE ICE CREAM

Serves: 4-6 • Prep Time: 30 minutes

ingredients

- 1 cup toasted coconut almond milk (or your favorite almond milk)
- ¾ cup cane sugar
- Pinch salt
- 1 can coconut milk
- 1 tablespoon vanilla

instructions:

Combines milks. Add salt and sugar to milks until dissolved. Stir, stir, stir. Add vanilla. Add mixture to ice cream maker. This ice cream is the most accurate, dairy free texture I've experienced. I love to add all sort of mix-ins in the final minutes of the freeze, before I move to the freezer.

Helpful Tip:

MIX IN IDEAS:

- ¼ cup chocolate chips melted with 1 teaspoon coconut oil, drizzled in while freezing.
- Graham crackers and marshmallow bits.
- The last gluten free recipe you made that crumbled apart.
- Oats and blueberries.
- Fresh fruit.
- Fruit jam.

VANILLA (COCONUT) PUDDING

Serves: 4-5 • Prep Time: 5 minutes • Cook Time: 15 minutes

ingredients

- ¾ cup organic cane sugar
- 2 tablespoons arrowroot
- ¼ teaspoon salt
- 2 cups canned coconut milk
- 2 slightly beaten egg yolks or 1 well-beated egg
- 2 tablespoons butter or coconut oil
- 1 teaspoon vanilla extract

Helpful Tip:

There are pre-made gluten free crusts out there, and this pudding poured right into one is the easiest "make and take" unexpected dessert surprises I know.

instructions:

1. In saucepan, blend sugar, arrowroot and salt; add coconut milk. Cook and stir over medium heat till thickened and bubbly. Cook and stir 2 minutes more. Remove from heat.
2. Stir small amount of hot mixture into yolks (or beaten egg); return to hot mixture; cook and stir 2 minutes more. Remove from heat; blend in coconut oil and vanilla. Pour in sherbet dishes; chill.

CHOCOLATE VARIATION: Follow directions for vanilla pudding. Add ¼ cup melted chocolate chips along with the coconut milk.

COCONUT VARIATION: Stir in ¼ cup toasted coconut, sprinkle more toasted coconut on top when serving.

Helpful Tip:

I like to serve this on top of shortbread or gluten free graham crackers pressed into crust, mixed with just enough coconut oil to bind. Can be topped with toasted coconut. Also great as a fruit dip or frozen as popsicles.

CINNAMON APPLES

Serves: 2 • Prep Time: 3 minutes • Cook Time: 15-20 minutes

● **PALEO** ● GRAIN-FREE ● **GUT HEALTH**

Easiest little sweet treat, ever! I LOVE to have these as a simple snack. We love to put these over ice cream, eat as an applesauce or have even added them to the simple ice cream at the end of freezing. Yum town. The pectin that is produced by the apple skins in the cooking process is a helpful prebiotic for the GI tract and gently binds to heavy metals - bonus points for gut health! This is a gentle, helpful binder when given to children, 1-2 tablespoons, consistently.

ingredients

- 2 organic apples, washed, cored, deseeded, NOT deskinned
- 2 tablespoons coconut oil
- 2 tablespoons ground cinnamon
- Pinch salt

instructions:

1. Preheat skillet over medium.
2. Core and chop apples in slices or a large dice.
3. Add coconut oil to skillet to melt.
4. Add apples. Cook 3-5 minutes until browning has begun. Add cinnamon and cook until apples are your desired texture, approximately 5-10 minutes longer. Add salt. Continuing to cook low and slow will allow the natural sugars to release an caramelize a bit more. As soon as the apple skins have a sheen about them and are no longer very firm, the pectin has released and you can remove from the heat.

OATMEALS AFTER SCHOOLS

Serves: 18 cookies • Prep Time: 10 minutes • Cook Time: 12-14 minutes

ingredients

- 2 eggs
- ½ cup coconut sugar
- ¼ cup softened coconut oil
- ½ teaspoon vanilla extract
- ½ teaspoon baking powder
- 1 ½ cups oats
- 3 tablespoons coconut flour
- ⅓ cup chocolate chips or raisins

instructions:

1. Turn oven to 350°F. Line a baking sheet with parchment paper.
2. Cream together eggs, coconut sugar, coconut oil and vanilla extract.
3. Add oats, coconut flour. Allow mixture to sit for 5 minutes to allow coconut flour to absorb liquid.
4. Stir in chocolate chips or raisins.
5. Scoop onto baking sheet using 1 ½ tablespoon cookie scoop. Cookies will not spread. Once scooped, use the bottom of a mason jar to press cookie down.
6. Bake for 12-14 minutes or just until bottom edges begin to brown.

TIP: I like to sprinkle a bit of cinnamon on top of the raisin version and a dash of crunchy salt on top of the chocolate chip version.

LEMON BARS

Serves: 12 • Prep Time: 10 minutes • Cook Time: 50 minutes

● GRAIN-FREE

ingredients

- For the Crust:
    - ¾ cup coconut flour
    - ½ cup arrowroot powder
    - ½ cup ghee **or** coconut oil, melted
    - ¼ cup monk fruit sweetener **or** coconut sugar
    - ½ teaspoon pure vanilla extract
    - ½ teaspoon sea salt
    - 2 pasture-raised eggs

- For the Filling:
    - 9 pasture-raised eggs
    - 1 cup freshly squeezed lemon juice
    - ¾ cup raw local honey
    - 6 tablespoons arrowroot powder
    - 1 tablespoon finely grated lemon zest
    - ½ teaspoon fine sea salt

instructions:

1. Preheat over to 350°F and lightly grease a 9 by 13-inch baking dish with coconut oil or ghee.
2. To begin making crust, combine the coconut flour, arrowroot powder, coconut oil, monk fruit or coconut sugar, vanilla extract, and salt. Add the eggs and whisk until the eggs are fully incorporated and a loose dough forms.
3. Press the dough into the bottom of the baking dish, making sure to press the dough slightly up the sides of the dish so the lemon filling does not end up seeping beneath crust. Bake in the oven for 15 minutes.
4. Next, in a blender, combine the eggs, lemon juice, honey, arrowroot powder, lemon zest, and sea salt until thoroughly mixed.
5. Pour the filling onto the hot crust and return the dish to the oven to continue baking for another 15 minutes, or until the center is almost set but still jiggles a bit.
6. Turn off the heat and cool in the oven with the door cracked open for 20 minutes.
7. Allow to chill completely in the refrigerator (preferably overnight) before serving. Slice into bars or squares and serve topped with berry jam.

FRUIT CRISP

Serves: 6-8 • Prep Time: 10 minutes • Cook Time: 30-40 minutes

This recipe was made famous by Shauna Niequist in one of her fabulous books. I've gone back and forth on sharing it here, think I love it too much and count on it far too often for so many quick gatherings that you, too, must know about it and all the ways I bend it to fit seasonal fruits. It's somehow even more magical the next day served with a bit of yogurt for breakfast.

ingredients

- 4 cups blueberries, cherries, peaches, apples or a mixture of complimentary fruits
- Crisp topping
    - 1 cup old fashioned oats
    - ½ cup chopped pecans
    - ½ cup almond meal
    - ¼ cup maple syrup
    - ¼ cup olive oil or avocado oil
    - ¼ teaspoon salt

instructions:

1. Pre-heat oven to 350°F. Lightly oil a 8 by 8-inch oven safe dish.
2. Layer fruit on bottom of pan. When using apples, I season with 1-2 teaspoons of cinnamon and 1-2 tablespoons coconut sugar. With blueberries, I often add lemon zest. Cherries get a teaspoon of vanilla or almond extract. The point here is to season your fruit a bit to build flavor. The inside of a vanilla bean, scraped out, is another decadent addition.
3. Mix together all ingredients in the crisp topping, then spread evenly on top of fruit.
4. Bake in oven until fruit bubbles and the topping is crisp and golden.